LUIS PALAU

Evangelist to the World

Ellen Bascuti

BARBOUR
PUBLISHING, INC.
Uhrichsville, Ohio

Other books in the "Heroes of the Faith" series:

Brother Andrew
Gladys Aylward
William and Catherine Booth
John Bunyan
William Carey
Amy Carmichael
George Washington Carver
Fanny Crosby
Frederick Douglass
Jonathan Edwards
Jim Elliot
Charles Finney
Billy Graham
C. S. Lewis
Eric Liddell
David Livingstone
Martin Luther

D. L. Moody
Samuel Morris
George Müller
Watchman Nee
John Newton
Florence Nightingale
Francis and Edith Schaeffer
Mary Slessor
Charles Spurgeon
Hudson Taylor
William Tyndale
Corrie ten Boom
Mother Teresa
Sojourner Truth
John Wesley
George Whitefield

©2000 by Ellen Bascuti.

ISBN 1-57748-803-2

All Scripture quotations, unless otherwise indicated, are taken from the HOLY BIBLE, NEW INTERNATIONAL VERSION®. NIV®. Copyright © 1973, 1978, 1984 by International Bible Society. Used by permission of Zondervan Publishing House. All rights reserved.

Scripture quotations marked RSV are taken from the Revised Standard Version of the Bible, copyright 1946, 1952, 1971 by the Division of Christian Education of the National Council of the Churches of Christ in the USA. Used by permission.

Scripture verses marked NKJV are taken from the New King James Version. Copyright © 1979, 1980, 1982 by Thomas Nelson, Inc. Used by permission. All rights reserved.

Scripture quotations marked TLB are taken from *The Living Bible* copyright © 1971. Used by permission of Tyndale House Publishers, Inc., Wheaton, Illinois 60189. All rights reserved.

Published by Barbour Publishing, Inc., P.O. Box 719, Uhrichsville, OH 44683
http://www.barbourbooks.com

Cover illustration © Dick Bobnick.

Member of the
Evangelical Christian
Publishers Association

Printed in the United States of America.

LUIS
PALAU

Dedication

To my favorite companion, ultimate encourager,
and wonderful husband:
You were right, Mihai. I can do it!

one

The plane lurched again. Clutching the armrests on his seat, Luis Palau hoped that the old DC-6 would still be in one piece by the time it reached America. Leaning back in his seat, he smoothed imaginary wrinkles from the jacket of his new black suit and tried to relax. *There's no reason to be nervous, Palau,* he told himself. *You're twenty-five years old. This may be your first flight, but there's nothing to it.*

His silent pep talk was undermined by the somersaults his stomach was performing as the plane chugged over the Andes Mountains. Finally, his queasiness abated as the DC-6 settled in at a lower altitude to take the strain off the engines. Luis sighed, thinking of the adventure that was taking him away from his family and friends in Argentina to the unfamiliar territory of California. Even loneliness and a stomachache could not lessen his excitement.

God has given me this opportunity to travel to America,

Luis reflected. *He gave me this dream to see more of the world and broaden my understanding of other countries. He wants me to use my time in the States to become a better evangelist; to help me as I tell others about Him. I'm finally on my way!*

Settling into the seat cushion, Luis began to think about home, his father and mother, and the events that God had used to develop his heart for evangelism.

Luis was born on November 27, 1934, the firstborn—and only son—of Luis Palau Sr., a well-to-do businessman who had his own construction company, and his wife, Matilde. Although Luis Sr. believed in God and Jesus Christ, They had no place in his daily life. When he brought his namesake to be christened at the local Catholic church—the only church in the town of Ingeniero-Maschwitz, a province of Buenos Aires—Mr. Palau was merely following religious tradition.

Luis's mother, on the other hand, regularly attended church and played the organ in the local parish. But those activities couldn't fill the hole in her heart. Something was missing. But what? She didn't know if she would ever discover the answer.

Not long after Luis was christened, his parents met Edward Rogers, a British executive with the Shell Oil Company in Argentina. Rogers and his wife never missed an opportunity to tell others about Jesus Christ. Soon after befriending the Palaus, Mr. Rogers gave them a copy of the Gospel of Matthew.

Mrs. Palau began to read this portion of the Bible, always kneeling out of reverence for the Scriptures. One day she read, "Blessed are the pure in heart, for they will see God" (Matthew 5:8).

I know my heart isn't pure, she thought. *But I want it to be. I won't settle for anything less.* With the help of Mr. and Mrs. Rogers, Mrs. Palau prayed and trusted Jesus Christ as her Lord and Savior. At last she had discovered the answer for which she had long been searching.

Mrs. Palau and little Luis began attending the Christian Brethren church—which met in a small metal shed—where Mr. Rogers sometimes preached. Mr. Palau refused to go with her. "I don't want anything to do with this evangelical stuff," he said. But sometimes at night he would stand outside the small chapel and listen to the Bible lessons.

"Will you come to church with me today?" Mrs. Palau asked her husband one morning.

For once, Mr. Palau agreed, though reluctantly. The couple sat together, with eighteen-month-old Luis between them. As Mr. Palau listened to Mr. Rogers speak, and as he remembered the words he had heard during his secret chapel visits, he knew that God wanted him to make a decision. Would he accept or reject God's gift to him of salvation through Jesus Christ?

No one in that congregation would ever forget what happened next. In the middle of the sermon, Mr. Palau stood and interrupted the pastor. Using a statement often made by Christians at that time in Argentina, he said, "I receive Jesus Christ as my only and sufficient Savior." With that declaration, he sat down.

From that day forward, Luis's father became a bold witness for Jesus Christ. Almost every weekend, Mr. Palau and others from the church would pile into one of the trucks from his construction business, drive to a surrounding town, and tell as many people as possible about Jesus Christ.

One morning, when Luis was a school-age boy, his

father said, "Come ride with me today, Luisito."

Luis climbed eagerly into the back of the truck and sat on a bench. When they got to the town where they were going to evangelize, his father handed him some tracts and said, "You can help us pass these out." Luis soon joined the rest of the group as they sang and tossed tracts to the people walking or standing on the side of the road. He quickly learned that not everyone wanted to hear about salvation through Jesus Christ. With eyes wide and heart pounding, Luis listened to the laughter, the insults, and the name-calling. Several times, he had to dodge a well-aimed stone. Nevertheless, week after week, Mr. Palau kept passing out tracts, and that made Luis proud.

Soon Mr. Palau became an elder in the church, often preaching in the new chapel he had helped to build. Luis always listened closely when his father spoke. Then, during the week, Luis would assemble his sisters to play church. "I'll be the preacher," he told them, "and you can sing and listen to me speak." As he preached, Luis tried to emulate his father's gestures, voice, and words.

One brisk winter morning, Luis woke early to the sound of his father starting a fire in the woodstove. He climbed out of bed and crept down the stairs to watch. Soon, Mr. Palau walked into his office study, wrapped himself in a poncho, and dropped to his knees to read his Bible and pray. *My dad is talking to God,* Luis realized. When his father began getting ready for work, Luis climbed back upstairs and crawled into bed, feeling warm and thankful for having a godly father.

On another occasion, Mr. Palau called Luis aside. "Reading the Bible is important, Luisito," he said. "I read a chapter from Proverbs every day, since Proverbs has thirty-one chapters and there are thirty-one days in most months." When Luis grew older, he began to put his father's words into practice—a pattern he still keeps.

In Luis's eyes, his father was everything a man should be. He was honest and well-respected in the church and community, yet humble and quiet. Luis wanted to be just like him. But it seemed that no matter how hard he tried, Luis couldn't control his quick temper or sharp tongue. Every time something went wrong, he exploded in anger. If he felt he had been treated unfairly in a soccer game, he would use some of the worst language on the field. He would shout and say the meanest things he could think of to his family and friends.

After one such outburst, his parents locked Luis in the bathroom, hoping to cool his hot temper. Minutes later, he had an idea. *If I let the water run, they have to let me out,* he reasoned. Instead, he landed himself in the corner, staring at the wall. Eventually, his ugly and bitter thoughts would subside and his anger and explosiveness would disappear. . .until the next time he didn't get his way.

Luis always enjoyed the Christmas season. He loved the beautifully decorated tree that reached to the ceiling of their house, and he and his family always attended the Christmas Eve service at the church. Afterward, friends would come over and talk for hours. On Christmas morning, after hurrying through breakfast, he and his sisters would open their presents. After a while, they would go through the neighborhood and invite the other children over for tea. Then Mr. Palau would hand out gifts and tell the Christmas story. The night would end with a visit from the relatives.

During one holiday celebration, Luis looked outside and

noticed a gathering of neighbors outside the house. "What are they doing?" he asked his parents.

"They are performing a purifying ceremony," his father replied. "Because we are Protestants, they think we are a blight on the community."

Luis couldn't understand the neighbors' scorn. *I'm proud to be a Palau,* he told himself, *even if people think we're heretics.*

When Luis was old enough, he began to attend public school. Here, too, he was often teased because he was the only child of evangelical Christians at the school. Even the teachers would call him names, and they made him kneel in the corner on corn kernels if he misbehaved.

After one particularly rough day at school, Luis began to think about a story his mother had told him and his sisters. She often read biographies of missionaries to them in the evenings. His favorites were Mildred Cable and Francesca French, who had traveled together throughout Asia (particularly the Gobi Desert) to spread the gospel, despite tremendous persecution and physical abuse. Even though he had not yet made a decision to trust Jesus Christ, Luis thought, *If they can be treated so horribly and stand strong, so can I. I may be hated, but I will wear that badge with honor.*

When Luis was seven, his father decided to send him to Quilmes Preparatory School, a private British boarding school near Buenos Aires. "This way, Luis," Mr. Palau said, "you will receive the best possible education. Because lessons are taught in both English and Spanish, you will become fluent in both languages. Perhaps one day you will study at Cambridge University in England."

The entire family went along to drop off Luis at school. He couldn't wait to arrive, yet he wanted the ride to last forever. Because Quilmes was about forty miles from Ingeniero-Maschwitz, he couldn't go home every day after classes. He would have to live at the school with fifty other boys. And he would have to speak English. *I hope my poor English won't get me in trouble right away,* he thought.

The days at Quilmes flew by. Luis made friends quickly and it didn't take long for him to improve his English. And he enjoyed his classes, sports, and other activities. But the nights, at first, seemed unending. He often grabbed his Bible and flashlight and pulled the blankets over his head. When his three roommates asked what he was doing, Luis replied, "I'm reading." But under the covers, his eyes were filled with tears.

Luis soon adjusted to life at school, but he always looked forward to the weekends at home and summer vacation (which, in Argentina, begins in the middle of December). During those visits, Luis and his father talked at length and planned for the future.

When summer ended, eight-year-old Luis headed back to Quilmes full of stories. "Guess what I did this summer?" he asked his buddies. "My dad bought a new truck, and he let me drive it. Okay, sure, he was sitting right beside me, but I got to steer and everything. He even let me crawl under the hood and fix the engine." Luis didn't tell them that all he could do was check the oil and then try to get the dipstick back in.

Another time, he told them how his dad had treated him like a man by letting him sip maté, green tea, with the working men during their breaks.

Quilmes soon became like a new home to Luis and was good preparation for St. Alban's College, where he would go when he was ten years old. Shortly after his tenth birthday, Luis took all his final exams at Quilmes and began to prepare for the trip home. As he packed, he thought, *Summer's finally here. I can do whatever I want—plant vegetables and flowers in the plot of land Dad gave me, spend time with my friends, help Dad with his business. . .* His summer plans were interrupted by a phone call.

"It's your grandmother," he was told.

Luis knew immediately that something was wrong. Although his grandmother lived only a few streets away from Quilmes, school rules dictated that relatives could not call or visit the students. Hurrying to the phone, he picked up the receiver. "Grandma?"

"Luis," she said, not even saying hello or asking how he was doing, "your dad is very sick. We really have to pray for him."

As he hung up the phone, Luis had a terrible feeling. *My dad is dying,* he thought. The next morning, December 17, 1944, his grandmother came to put him on a train bound for home.

"It's serious," she said. "Your mom wants you to come and see your dad."

Boarding the train, Luis couldn't shake the feeling that his father was already gone.

two

Luis sat in silence on the train. He stared at the passing scenery, yet saw nothing. Nothing could ease the dread he felt in his heart. He was certain that he would arrive too late to say good-bye to his father. *How could anything be wrong with Dad?* Luis thought. *He doesn't get sick. He's my dad!*

Luis didn't even know what was wrong with his father. Later he would learn that Luis Sr. had contracted bronchial pneumonia and had suffered for ten days. He needed penicillin, but in December 1944 the antibiotic was all being sent to Europe and the Pacific to help soldiers wounded in World War II.

When the train finally reached Ingeniero-Maschwitz, Luis jumped out of his seat and pressed up against the door. He bounded down the steps and ran down the road, one thought keeping pace with his footfalls: *I have to get home. I have to get home.* The blast-furnace temperature didn't deter him, but the sight of people lounging around, sipping soft drinks, and fanning themselves, almost made him stop in his tracks. *How can they behave like that?* Luis thought. *Something is terribly wrong at my house, yet people in town are lazing around.*

Luis was almost home when he heard something. *What's that noise?* he asked himself. It sounded like. . .yes, the traditional wailing had begun. The hope he had been harboring in the back of his mind shattered. "Why does God allow this?" some of his non-Christian aunts and uncles were moaning and crying and asking. "So many little children left without a father. Oh, what will Matilde do?"

Relatives tried to stop Luis as he ran through the gate and up to the house. He brushed past them and was in the door before his mother even knew he was there. Then he saw his father's body, yellow and bloated. His dad had died a few hours earlier, and his body had dehydrated.

Luis ran to him, ignoring his sisters Matilde, Martha, Ketty, and Margarita, and all the other relatives. His father was lying in bed, as if asleep. *I have to be strong,* Luis thought, but in the midst of all the crying and sobbing he began to shake. *I can't believe this! I will never talk with my father again. Papito, you look so terrible. Please, don't be dead. Please be all right.* Luis hugged him and kissed him, but he was gone.

Luis felt hands on his shoulders. He turned and saw his mother—stunned but not crying. "Luisito, Luisito," she said softly, pulling him away. "I must talk to you and tell you how it was."

She took him outside, and he tried to stifle his sobs while listening to her account. "When the doctors realized they weren't able to do anything else for him, we decided to call you so you could hurry home. It was obvious he was dying, and as we gathered around his bed, praying and trying to comfort him, he seemed to fall asleep. He was struggling to breathe, but suddenly he sat up and began to sing."

"Sing?" Luis asked. "Mama, is that true?"

"Papito began to sing," she repeated, " 'Bright crowns up there, bright crowns for you and me.' Then 'the palm of victory, the palm of victory.' He sang it three times, all the while clapping in time as you children did when you sang it in Sunday school.

"Then, when Papito could no longer hold up his head, he fell back on the pillow and said, 'I'm going to be with Jesus, which is far better.' " A short time after that, thirty-five-year-old Luis Palau Sr. went to be with the Lord.

As painful as it was to remember, Luis couldn't stop thinking about how his father had died. The picture his mother had painted—the singing, the clapping, the peacefulness—was so vivid that Luis almost felt as if he had been there. His father was so unlike the typical Latin American, where the dying person cries out in fear of going to hell. *At least my dad was sure of heaven,* Luis thought. *I know for a fact that he's up there with Jesus right now.*

Still, Luis's grief devastated him, and he was angry at everything and everyone. He hated to walk by his father's study. He locked the gate on the plot of land his father had given him. He didn't want to see anything that reminded him of his dad. In his mind, his world and his future had come to an end. *It's not fair,* Luis thought. *Why couldn't my father die in old age like everyone else?*

That night, would-be comforters crowded into the house and sat around drinking coffee and talking in whispers. Since the burial would take place the next day, relatives in distant towns were contacted and began arriving throughout the night. They slept wherever they could—in beds, chairs, and on the floor all over the house.

I wish I could leave, escape the horror of this night, Luis thought. *But I'm the man of the house now. I need to stay awake; I need to help my mother.* It wasn't long, however, before his eyes grew heavy. The trip and the trauma had gotten to him, and ten-year-old Luis fell into a fitful sleep.

That day, young Luis learned the harsh reality of death. His father had been there, and then was gone, and that was it.

When Luis awoke the next morning, his first thought was, *Today we bury my father.* He had determined during the night that he would be at the grave site and would toss the first clump of dirt onto his father's casket—this would be his way of saying good-bye.

It wasn't going to be easy, though. Luis's aunts herded the children into the kitchen as nearly two hundred adults left the house and piled into their vehicles for the twenty-minute drive to the cemetery in Escobar. Luis was fuming. *This is my father,* he thought. *And these people are trying to tell me that I can't say good-bye to him? Why? If anyone should be there, it's me. I loved him, and he loved me. There is no way on earth anyone is going to stop me.*

Luis heard the cars' engines start. He was desperate. *A bold run for it would never work,* he thought. *Too many adults are standing between me and the door. Besides, they are all watching me, wondering what stunt I'm going to pull.*

The vehicles were starting to leave. "Robbie," Luis whispered frantically to his cousin. "Distract my aunts. I'm getting out of here." Luis edged toward the open window while Robbie sneaked toward a group of girls. Robbie grabbed their hair and yanked hard. At their screams, Luis's aunts ran to pull Robbie away.

At the same time, Luis climbed out the window and raced toward the line of slowly moving cars and trucks. Panting, he reached the last truck in the line. It belonged to his uncle Ramon. At his uncle's nod, Luis climbed in the back of the truck and hid under some supplies, just as his aunt ran out the door, demanding to know where he was. Triumphantly, though tearfully, Luis rode to the burial.

When Luis and Ramon finally reached the grave site, Mr. Rogers was just finishing speaking. Luis waited at the edge of the crowd. One of his uncles gently placed his arm around Luis's shoulders as they listened to the words about heaven and eternity. As several men began lowering the casket into the ground, Luis broke free. He shot through the tangle of legs, squeezing past several adults to find himself at the edge of the grave. The six-foot hole looked bottomless. Before anyone could react, Luis grabbed a handful of soil. *Good-bye, Papito,* Luis thought, tossing the dirt onto the casket. He would never forget the dull, echoing thud.

three

The sight outside the window broke through Luis's thoughts. *How beautiful,* he thought as they flew over the Caribbean at about twenty thousand feet. "Look at all those little white boats," Luis said in his best English.

His seatmate leaned across to look. "Those are clouds, kid," he said.

A bit embarrassed, Luis stared out the window again. *I can't believe fifteen years have passed already since that long train ride from Quilmes. I don't think I'll ever forget that trip home.*

As the plane made yet another stop on its way to the States, Luis thought, *I believe Dad's death has had more impact on my ministry than anything else in my entire life, besides my own conversion to Jesus Christ. I can feel my heart almost bursting from my body when I preach the gospel. My wish and desire is that people get right with*

God, settle the big question, and die happy, knowing they will be with Jesus, just like I know Dad is.

For days on end after his father's death, Luis continually questioned his mother about heaven, the second coming of Jesus Christ, and the Resurrection. She answered her grief-stricken son and his sisters with the truths of the Bible, drilling the words of the Lord Jesus into them:

" 'Do not let your hearts be troubled. Trust in God; trust also in me. In my Father's house are many rooms; if it were not so, I would have told you. I am going there to prepare a place for you. And if I go and prepare a place for you, I will come back and take you to be with me that you also may be where I am' " (John 14:1–3).

Luis memorized that portion, along with the apostle Paul's words from 1 Thessalonians 4:13–14:

"Brothers, we do not want you to be ignorant about those who fall asleep, or to grieve like the rest of men, who have no hope. We believe that Jesus died and rose again and so we believe that God will bring with Jesus those who have fallen asleep in him."

His mother's teaching during those summer months settled his questions about eternity and heaven. He had no doubt that his father was in heaven with Jesus Christ.

As the summer drew to a close, Mrs. Palau began talking to Luis about attending St. Alban's College, which was connected with the Cambridge University Overseas Program.

"Mom," Luis said, "I really don't want to go. I know I was excited about school before, but now you need me here at home."

"Before he died, your dad decided to send you to St. Alban's," she replied. "It may be expensive, but he set aside the money, and I want to follow through with his wishes. Besides, I've already hired someone to manage the family business. He will know better than I what needs to be done." No one knew then that her decision would eventually prove disastrous for the family's finances.

The beginning of the school year found Luis at St. Alban's, a tough and exclusive Anglican school for boys. Every morning, he sat in classes taught in Spanish. The rest of the day, different lessons were taught in English. If things went as planned, Luis would complete his studies in four years (equivalent to eight years of study for the average Argentinean student) and be qualified for graduate work at Cambridge University.

Luis soon learned the meaning of the words *discipline* and *structure*. Sometimes he griped: "We all have to wear British private-school uniforms. We have to get up at the same time, make our beds, clean our areas, and comb our hair just so. Then we're told, 'Stand in line; march.' And if we don't obey our 'masters,' boy, do we get it! The cricket-bat punishment is the worst. I've never received it, but I've heard that you have to bend over, touch your toes, and wait for the 'swing and sting' of that massive, flat bat." Secretly, however, Luis was proud of his school.

Schoolwork took up much of his time. He maintained fairly good grades, even with his bad attitude. "I'll study when I want to," he insisted, "and not just because the professor says I have to." And, as most boys do, he found time for shenanigans. Teachers and students alike had to beware of pranks, jokes, or traps. Anything and anyone was fair game.

Most of all, Luis enjoyed athletics. Cricket and rugby were the sports of choice at school—at least by the British.

But Luis preferred soccer. The one problem was that Latin America's number one sport was considered improper and was prohibited on campus.

Then, as now, school rules stand little chance against a boy's heart. Throughout the day, whispers could be heard, "Today at four o'clock. Pass it on." At the appointed time, Luis, along with other daring classmates, would gather behind a grove of trees on the edge of the school grounds. There, he imagined himself winning the World Cup with a spectacular last-second goal.

Still, all the activities could not keep Luis from feeling the effects of his father's death. *At least on the playing field I don't have to think about the future,* Luis told himself. *It seems like every day one of my aunts or uncles tells me I'm the man of the family and expects me to take over the family business someday and care for my mother and sisters. I'm only eleven years old. How can I handle these heavy responsibilities? More than that, how can I even think of running Dad's business when it brings back such painful memories?*

When Luis returned home for the summer, he realized that the family business was no longer what it had been when his father was alive. Several times his mother said, "Luis, I'm not sure we have the money to send you back to St. Alban's."

"I've got to go back," Luis whispered to himself. "St. Alban's is where I belong. If I stay here, I'll have to face all the awesome responsibilities that come with being the man of the family."

Although worried about his family's dwindling finances, Luis found one good thing about it: He now had a good

23

excuse not to attend summer camp. At least he thought it would work when Charles Cohen, one of his teachers at St. Alban's, asked him once again to go on a two-week camping trip up in the mountains along with several dozen other boys. Luis thought the trip sounded like fun, but he didn't want to give up part of his summer vacation at home. Besides, Mr. Cohen was one of the few evangelicals in the Anglican school, and when he took boys on camping trips, several usually came back as new Christians.

Someone will definitely put pressure on me to receive Jesus Christ, Luis thought. *I like things the way they are. I can quote Bible verse after Bible verse. I can sing the songs. I'll even say a prayer if someone asks. That's good enough for now.*

But Luis's plan backfired. Mr. Cohen said, "Money is no problem, Palau. I'll pay your way."

When Luis told his mother, she said, "I'm glad you're going, Luis. I'm just not sure you are a real, born-again Christian."

"Mom, come on," Luis said, rolling his eyes.

"No, Luis, I know what I'm saying," she replied. "I remember when you were three or four, you knelt beside me as I was praying for you. I said, 'Lord, I pray that Luisito will truly come to know You.' You looked at me and said, 'But Mommy, I do know the Lord Jesus.' You say the same thing now. You may know about Jesus and you may love Him, but you do not know Him in a personal way."

Luis knew there was no way out. In a few months, he would leave for camp. It annoyed him that he had been caught and forced to go—which was not the "in" thing for twelve-year-olds to do. Even his buddies refused to go. But Luis wasn't going to worry about camp now. He still had

24

most of the summer in front of him, which meant helping out with the family business.

The sun warmed Luis's shoulders as he sat in the truck. *This is the life,* Luis thought. *Driving around with a twenty-year-old who works for the family, delivering a load of cement bags. I think I've achieved manhood.*

Suddenly, the driver pulled over to the side of the road and pulled a magazine from his pocket.

Curious, Luis tried to see what it was. No, he would just have to wait.

The man then said, "Luisito, since you are becoming a young man now and you have no father, you need someone to talk to you about the facts of life."

Luis's heart began to pound. He had been pestering his mother to tell him about girls, sexuality, birth, and so on. Having heard the older boys at school talk made him as curious as any twelve-year-old boy. But his mother kept telling him that he would have to wait until he was thirteen. *Now I'm going to get some straight answers from someone who really knows the score,* Luis thought.

"I want to make a man of you," the man continued. But instead of saying anything more, he simply opened his magazine and turned the pages.

Luis stared in disbelief, shocked that anyone would show him something so revealing. *How disgusting,* Luis thought. But he couldn't take his eyes off the page. He knew it was all wrong; it was dirty; it wasn't pure; yet he was curious. He wanted to see it, yet he hated it.

After flipping through its fifty or sixty pages, the driver tucked the magazine back in his pocket and continued with the delivery.

Luis couldn't stop thinking about those pictures. He

knew that if the driver asked him the next day if he wanted to see the magazine, he would run the other way. He felt guilty and sinful. *Why couldn't I look away?* he wondered. *Will God judge me for my thoughts?*

Luis didn't know that his reactions were hardly unique among twelve-year-old boys who'd had their first shocking encounter with pornography. All he knew was that he couldn't push those images out of his mind. *Maybe I can escape these thoughts at camp,* Luis hoped.

four

Luis jumped out of bed. The day had finally arrived. Soon he would be trekking off to Azul, a hilly, mountainous area where the Christian camp was located. He hoped his excitement about his first camping experience would help him forget about the sins of his mind and the accompanying dreadful feeling in the pit of his stomach.

At the camp, Luis recognized most of the boys from St. Alban's. "Look, Luis," they called, "we're going to sleep in Argentine army tents. Did you bring your cot?"

Luis joined the fifty or sixty other boys as they set up the tents, dug trenches around them, policed the area, and were taught how to "rough it." Counselors from different missionary organizations supervised the activities.

"There's Mr. Cohen," someone whispered. When Luis looked up, he saw the stiff, curt, formal, aloof teacher from St. Alban's, in khaki shorts, cracking jokes, acting almost as if he were on their level.

"It's time for the Bible lesson, boys," one of the counselors called. The campers gathered around as an American Bible teacher spoke on purity. Luis listened carefully. He still felt bad about his own confused thoughts on sex, but this man gave him hope. *He knows what he's talking about,* Luis thought. *Maybe he's not giving me the detailed instruction about sex that I need, but he's shown me you can be a pure man in an impure world. Those images in my mind may be attractive, but they're not right. I am going to model myself after pure Christian men.*

Luis was beginning to like camp, although he missed the contact with the outside world. Sometimes he complained to his fellow campers, "No radios, no newspapers, no nothing. We can't even hear the soccer scores." The time was filled instead with Bible memorization, singing, and the usual fun and games. But Luis knew that soon someone was going to confront him about his faith.

He watched it happen every evening. Each counselor had about ten boys in his tent, and each night one boy was taken for a walk and given the opportunity to say yes or no to Christ's claims upon his life.

When the last night of camp arrived, Luis knew his turn had come. Every other boy in his tent had talked with their counselor, Frank Chandler. Luis lay on his cot in the dark tent, thinking. *I wish I could run and hide. I'm so embarrassed that I haven't received Christ yet. Maybe I could lie and say I have. No, I can't do that. I feel so guilty for my sins, but I just don't want to make a decision yet. I know, I'll pretend I'm asleep, and maybe Frank will go away.*

When Frank walked into the tent, Luis closed his eyes and quieted his breathing. "Come on, Luis, get up," Frank said. "I want to talk to you. Come on, up!"

Luis did not move. Even with eyes closed, he saw Frank's flashlight shine on his face. Still Luis continued his act. All of a sudden, he felt the cot tilt as Frank picked up the bed and dumped Luis onto the ground. Frank had known all along that Luis was faking. Rubbing his eyes and still feigning sleepiness, Luis slipped on his canvas-topped shoes and a jacket.

Frank and Luis walked outside and sat down on a fallen tree. Luis was cold and felt tiny raindrops tickle his face and hands. A thunderstorm was coming their way. Frank pulled out his flashlight again and opened his New Testament. "Luis," he asked, "are you a born-again Christian or not?"

"I don't think so," Luis replied.

"Well, it's not a matter of whether you think so or not. Are you or aren't you?"

"No, I'm not."

"If you died tonight," Frank asked, "would you go to heaven or hell?"

Luis sat quietly for a moment, a bit taken back, and then said, "I'm going to hell."

"Is that where you want to go?"

"No," he replied.

"Then why are you going there?"

Luis shrugged his shoulders. "I don't know."

Frank then turned in his Bible to the Book of Romans and read: "If you confess with your lips, Luis, that Jesus is Lord and believe in your heart, Luis, that God raised him from the dead, you, Luis, will be saved. For man believes with his heart and so is justified, and he confesses with his lips and so is saved" (see Romans 10:9–10 RSV).

Frank looked back at him. "Luis, do you believe in your heart that God raised Jesus from the dead?"

"Yes, I do."

"Then what do you have to do next to be saved?"

Luis hesitated. The rain began to fall harder.

"Read what the Bible says, Luis."

Luis leaned over and read Romans 10:9 once more. "If you confess with your lips that Jesus is Lord. . .you will be saved."

"Luis, are you ready to confess Him as your Lord right now?"

"Yes."

"All right; let's pray," Frank said as he slipped his arm around Luis.

Out in the rain, sitting on a log, Luis made his decision to open his heart to Christ. He prayed, "Lord Jesus, I believe You were raised from the dead. I confess You with my lips. Give me eternal life. I want to be Yours. Save me from hell. Amen."

With tears running down his cheeks, Luis gave Frank a big hug. Then, soaking wet from the rain, they ran back into the tent. Luis crawled into bed, so excited he could hardly sleep. He grabbed his flashlight, pulled the blanket over his head, and wrote in his Bible, "February 12, 1947" and "I received Jesus Christ."

I may be only twelve years old, Luis thought, *but I know I'm born again. I'm saved. I'm a member of the family of God. I have eternal life because Jesus Christ said, " 'I give them eternal life, and they shall never perish; no one can snatch them out of my hand' " (John 10:28). No other decision I make can be as important as choosing eternal life with Jesus.*

When Luis returned home and told his mother about his decision, she was ecstatic. His own excitement lasted several months and, when school began, he shared his nighttime camp experience with his friends. But they didn't share Luis's enthusiasm. They were still telling dirty stories and pulling practical jokes—things Luis now refused to participate in. "Come on, Palau, not you, too. Snap out of it!" they told him.

Luis didn't listen. His life had changed. He began carrying his Bible with him a lot and would study it every day. The required weekly attendance at church took on a whole new meaning for him. He sang in the choir, until his terrible voice got him kicked out. He became a much better student. And he pitched in to help at Crusader youth group meetings held in Mr. Cohen's home on Sunday afternoons—Luis sang out, listened hard, and studied all his Bible lessons.

That year, the Crusader Club was visited by two old missionary ladies, Mildred Cable and Francesca French, who had spent years spreading the gospel in China. He listened intently as they told tremendous stories of their travels through the Gobi Desert, and of being dragged through the streets of pagan cities because they insisted upon sharing Christ with the Chinese.

Luis could hardly believe their tales of courage. He prayed, "God, I thought I was an outspoken Christian, but what am I doing compared to these two women? They gave up the luxuries of life to minister under terrible conditions, just because they love You and want to serve You. Lord, help me love You like that."

One day, several months later, Luis stepped off the streetcar and headed toward home. Crusaders had been interesting, and he couldn't wait to get home to tell his mother what Mr. Cohen had taught them that day. Then he looked down at his empty hands. "My Bible," he yelled, and ran back the way he had come. The streetcar with his Bible was long gone. Without his Bible, Luis no longer spent time every day in God's Word. He quit attending Crusaders. He lost his excitement over Bible classes and almost everything else that went along with his commitment to Christ. Luis still loved and believed and respected the gospel, but he wasn't going to let it interfere with his life.

What brought about this quick turnoff? It may have had to do with some punishment Luis received at the hands of Mr. Cohen, who was the teacher in charge of campus order on that fateful day.

Luis was in art class and doing none too well. His painting looked nothing like a tree, but his antics, meant to impress his friends, brought satisfactory results. After one particularly rowdy outburst, Mr. Thompson, the new art teacher walked over. He took a puff from his distinguished-looking pipe and made a rather sarcastic remark about Luis's horrible painting.

As the teacher walked away, Luis responded with a foul word in Spanish, assuming that Mr. Thompson, who had recently arrived from England, wouldn't understand it. The rest of the class, however, understood Luis just fine and laughed.

"What did you say, Palau?" the teacher asked.

"Oh, nothing, Mr. Thompson, sir. Nothing, really."

"No, what was it, Palau?"

"It was really nothing important, sir."

"I'd really like to hear it again, Palau. Would you mind repeating it?"

"Oh, I don't think it's worth repeating. I. . ."

"All right," Mr. Thompson snapped. "Go see the master on duty."

The class fell silent. Luis couldn't believe that one word from his mouth had gotten him in such deep trouble. *Now I have to tell the master on duty why I was sent to him,* Luis thought as he walked out of the classroom. *I wonder who's on duty?*

He almost died inside when he saw Mr. Cohen in the office.

"Come in, Palau," he said. "Why are you here?"

"Mr. Thompson sent me."

"Is that so? Why?"

Luis thought, *Why is Mr. Cohen being so terribly cold? We know each other and have spent a lot of time together at camp and at Crusaders. He's even a fellow Christian, but here he is, aloof and frigid again.*

"Why?" Mr. Cohen asked again.

"I said a bad word," Luis confessed.

"Repeat it."

"Oh, I had better not."

"Repeat it," Mr. Cohen insisted.

There's no way out, Luis thought. *One little word in art class. And now all this.* Luis told Mr. Cohen what he had said, then waited as Mr. Cohen sat without moving. *Come on; do something, Don't just stare at me. I know you're disappointed and disgusted with me.*

As Mr. Cohen reached for the cricket bat, he finally spoke. "You know, Palau, I'm going to give you six of the best."

Luis froze. That was the maximum number of swats for any punishment.

"Bend and touch your toes, please."

As Luis slowly bent over, Mr. Cohen said, "Before I punish you, I want to tell you this, Palau. You are the greatest hypocrite I have ever seen in my life. You think you get away with your arrogant, cynical, above-it-all, know-it-all attitude, but I have watched you. You come to Bible class, all right, but you are a hypocrite." Then Mr. Cohen began to swing.

The physical punishment stung for days. Luis's sore seat made it hard to sit down, and he slept on his stomach for a week. He cried and cried, even though he tried to be tough about it.

But the effect of Mr. Cohen's words lasted much longer. For months, Luis hated the man, refusing to look at him, let alone say hello or smile at him. He quit paying attention in Mr. Cohen's Bible classes, and he quit going to Crusaders. And if St. Alban's hadn't required his attendance, Luis would have quit going to church, too.

Something had soured the sweet relationship between him and God. Luis started to stretch the limits placed on him by his school, his mother, and the church. The things that he felt were sinful—attending school dances, reading magazines about car racing, and playing sports on Sunday— he did anyway. He joined his old friends with their life of parties and soccer games, began talking rough again, and generally developed a bad attitude toward life.

Luis felt worldly, sinful, guilty, and a bit afraid. *What's going to become of me?* he wondered. *I want to be a good Christian, but I don't know how.* His bubble of excitement had burst. Reading the Bible, praying, and going to church— things that used to thrill him—now became boring. *I know I'm a Christian,* he told himself, *but I don't want to be considered a fool.*

Luis decided to let the other Christians at St. Alban's take a stand for Christ. He would do his own thing, live how he pleased.

One day, Mrs. Palau told her son, "The business is failing. The person I hired to manage it cheated us and left us without any money. We're virtually penniless."

Luis was furious. How could someone jeopardize the survival of a widow and her children? *If only I could get my hands on him. . .*

Mrs. Palau's words broke through Luis's thoughts. "I'm doing everything possible to see that you remain in school. Because you are part British, a British charity has agreed to help pay for part of your tuition. But you'll need to live with your grandparents in Quilmes and commute to school to save money."

Luis felt humiliated. What would his friends at St. Alban's think? He began to boast, "I can't believe how well things are going. Business is booming; the money is just rolling in. Wait until I get back to run it. I'm going to be rich and powerful, a self-made businessman." He knew he was lying. The family was nearly bankrupt and the business was virtually finished. Luis began blaming God for most of his troubles, which helped ease the guilt he felt about doing his own thing.

The money finally ran out, and Mrs. Palau came to tell Luis that he could not continue at St. Alban's much longer. He could complete what would be the equivalent of a junior college degree in the United States, but he would not be able to take the last year and qualify for the graduate program at Cambridge. Continuing his education, a dream Luis had nurtured for years, was out of the question.

Luis began to work part-time for his British grandfather in his small business of selling sauces and smoked fish to restaurants. He needed to help support his family, who had moved several hundred miles north to Cordoba, now that there was nothing left of the business.

God has played a cruel joke on me, Luis thought. *Eight long, double years of schooling in the British boarding schools, and what am I left with? An intermediate degree, no money, and no future! I think I'm glad I haven't served God more. I deserve better than this, so why should I live for Him?*

Inside, Luis knew he was wrong. He just wished that he had the courage to return to full joy in Jesus.

No longer a student, Luis considered himself a real British man of the world. He joined the local university club and bought a pipe, not realizing that he was imitating Mr. Thompson, his old art teacher. He hung out with his non-Christian friends, using them as an excuse to do the things he considered wrong—going to soccer games on Sundays, fantasizing about girls, and wasting time. Those were about the worst things they could think of.

The desire to be "in," to be "cool," kept Luis following the crowd—until just before Carnival Week.

five

I n a few more hours, the plane would land at Miami Airport. *God has been with me on this trip,* Luis thought, *just as He's always been with me. I failed God many times—especially during those three final years at St. Alban's—but He never failed me.* Luis grabbed his Bible and turned to Philippians 1:6. He read, "I am sure that God who began the good work within you will keep right on helping you grow in his grace until his task within you is finally finished on that day when Jesus Christ returns" (TLB).

Carnival Week of 1952 had proved that verse true!

Luis's grandparents were gone for the weekend. He had the entire house to himself. The next day he and his friends would head out to the streets for the first day of Carnival Week—a celebration much like Mardi Gras in New Orleans. Because the festivities are followed by forty days of confession and penance, anything goes. People dress in costumes and masks and dance around the clock. It's a week of total abandonment. It's not unusual for a young person to experience his first night of drunkenness—or worse—during Carnival Week.

I thought I was looking forward to some excitement, Luis said to himself, *something more bizarre than the sophisticated little parties and games the university club offers. All the "fun" they offer is so meaningless and boring. But now, I'm not so sure. What if something snaps and I go off the deep end at a wild party? Could God ever forgive my out-and-out mockery of everything I've been taught?*

Luis was nearly panicking. If he didn't get out of Carnival Week, he would be swallowed up, finished, sunk. He knew the Bible said nothing could separate him from the love of God, but he was convinced that participating in the festival would officially sever his relationship with God. He had to get out of it.

Luis fell to his knees. "God," he prayed, "You know I don't have the guts to tell my friends I'm not going. I need some reason. Get me out of this, and I will give up everything that's of the world. I will serve You and give my whole life to You. Just get me out of this!"

The next morning Luis awoke on his back, then blinked until the ceiling came into focus. Slowly he sat up, swung his legs over the side of the bed, and sat there a moment. He yawned. *My mouth feels strange,* Luis thought. He touched it. It wasn't painful, but it was bloated.

He stumbled to the mirror and stared at his swollen mouth. *It looks like I tried to swallow a Ping-Pong ball.* Then he gave his reflection a crooked grin and said aloud,

"God has answered my prayer!"

He hurried to the phone and called up one of his friends. "I can't go to the dance tonight, and I won't be going to the carnival at all this week."

"Come on, Luis! Everything has been planned!"

"No. I have a good reason, and I will not go."

"I'm coming over," he insisted. "You must be crazy."

A few minutes later he showed up with three or four other guys and girls. They tried to convince Luis that the swelling would go down and that he should change his mind.

Luis resisted. He was too much of a coward to tell them the real reason he wasn't going, but his mind was made up. He no longer wanted anything to do with the fleeting pleasures the world offered. When his friends finally left, Luis went back into the house, broke his pipe in two, tore up his university club membership card, and ripped up all his soccer and car-racing magazines and many record albums.

The next day, he went to church morning and night. He had escaped Carnival Week and had returned to the Lord. His life had completely changed.

Not only did Luis take God more seriously, he now also took his responsibilities more seriously. *The time for fun and games is over,* Luis thought. *Now it's time to start a career.* Although only seventeen, Luis wanted a job that paid a good salary. He wanted to help support his mother and sisters, who were living hand-to-mouth in Cordoba. He applied at the Bank of London in Buenos Aires. Because of his bilingual British education, Luis was hired as a junior employee in training.

Luis worked hard and learned all he could about international banking. In a short time, he received a couple of promotions, mostly because he was bilingual. Although friendly with his coworkers, Luis refused to play the office games and join in the card games, drinking, parties, and all the rest. Instead, he thought about his future. Gone were the days of dreaming about becoming a race-car driver or soccer player. He was looking for the best way to change his world—perhaps by becoming a lawyer and protecting the poor and unfortunate people, especially widows and orphans.

Luis shared his dreams with his uncle, Jack Balfour, who was five years older. In the evenings, Luis and Jack, who lived in the same house, would walk and talk for hours, planning ways to make a difference in society. Luis had no idea that many of their brainstorms would become a reality in the years to come.

One day while studying the Bible, Luis came across an important truth. He told Jack, "There are so many things I want to see happen, things I want to do. I've realized that God has given me these ambitions. Reading John 14:12–15 assures me that God wants us to dream great dreams, plan great plans, pray great prayers, and obey God's great commands."

Another day, Luis read this remark by President Abraham Lincoln: "I shall prepare, and one day my chance will come." Luis was convinced of that for himself, as well. But first, he wanted to help his family.

As he prayed, Luis decided he should move north four hundred miles to Cordoba, where the Bank of London had a branch office. There he could be with his family, start over with new friends, and get his roots deep into a good church.

At that time, no one ever requested a transfer. But Luis,

sure his decision came from God, gathered his nerve, stopped by the personnel department, and filled out an application.

"God," Luis prayed, "they may fire me. But if this is Your way of getting me out of a situation You don't want me in, I'm willing to accept it."

That evening, Luis called home. "Mom, I've submitted an application for a transfer to Cordoba," he said, "but that doesn't mean I'll get it." When Luis hung up the phone, he was certain that his mother, who was thrilled with his decision, had already started praying.

Soon Luis received a memo to report to the personnel office. His determination to follow God's will wavered. "What a fool," he told himself. "You've been an idiot! These people have been good to you, and now you ask to be transferred to some remote branch office! Wait a minute, Palau. Even if the firing is painful and you have been stupid, it's a sacrifice for the Lord, and He will provide."

His resolve restored, Luis walked down the hall for his meeting.

"Why do you want to transfer to Cordoba?" the personnel manager asked.

"For two reasons," Luis said. "My mother and sisters live there and need me, and I know Cordoba has a good branch bank." He waited in uncomfortable silence for the personnel manager's decision.

"You know," he said, "it would be good for you. With a branch of that size, you could learn banking more quickly, because there are only one or two people in each major department. There won't be a jungle of people to go around.

"In fact, we'll put this down as if it were our idea, and

then we can justify paying for your move and giving you a promotion and raise."

Luis's mouth dropped open, but the personnel manager wasn't finished.

"If you progress as nicely there as you have here at head-quarters, within six months we'll put you in charge of foreign operations of that branch, and in a year we'll bring you back here for a few weeks of specialized training. In our eyes, you will begin as the number four man in Cordoba."

Luis was not yet eighteen years old.

A few weeks before leaving, Luis switched on the shortwave radio, then stretched out on the living room floor at his Uncle Arnold and Aunt Marjorie's home. He heard a vibrant, somewhat high-pitched, and excited voice. A preacher—Luis didn't catch his name—was calling men to come to Jesus Christ. Then he heard another man's strong, deep voice, singing a hymn to close the program.

The whole experience left him exhilarated. Sprawled across that floor, Luis prayed: "Jesus, someday use me on the radio to bring others to You, just as this program has firmed up my resolve to completely live for You." Later Luis realized he had been listening to Billy Graham and George Beverly Shea.

Little did he know that, in the years ahead, he would preach to tens of millions of people via the radio in the United States of America and around the world. God would honor the prayer of his youth.

Luis soon moved to Cordoba. The house his family rented seemed to shrink to the size of a shoe box when all seven members of the family squeezed into it. Even with Luis's good salary, they couldn't afford anything larger. So Luis turned the living room into his bedroom and slept on the sofa. With no extra money, new clothes were a luxury. So Luis made do with the few he owned—his uncle Arnold's discarded suits and his grandfather's old topcoats. Once in a while, extra money came in when an old business debt was paid by someone honest enough to look up the family and take care of it.

Mrs. Palau purchased whatever groceries they could afford from a small store near their home. Often all she bought was a loaf of French bread and a small tomato.

"Put this on your tab today?" the shopkeeper always asked, knowing that Mrs. Palau always paid him whenever she received any money.

"Yes," Mrs. Palau simply responded.

In the evenings, the family gathered for dinner. On the table sat her purchases—the makings for tomato sandwiches. "Let's pray," Mrs. Palau said, and she thanked God for His provision.

His mother's attitude taught Luis never to complain about the little they had. "God is teaching us to look to Him for every need," she told him. "We are experiencing the reality of Jesus' words in Matthew 6:33: 'But seek first his kingdom and his righteousness, and all these things will be given to you as well.' "

His first Sunday in Cordoba, Luis attended the local Christian Brethren assembly, a group of about 130 people and one of the biggest churches Luis had ever seen. He knew he wanted to be a part of this exciting program, run by the elders and full-time missionary George Mereshian, and said so.

"That's great, Luis," Mr. Mereshian told Luis. "As you know, our church holds fast to the rule that a person can't serve as a leader unless he has been baptized, served in lesser capacities, and studied God's Word in-depth for several years. I would like to be the person who disciples you, who helps you become the leader God wants you to be."

Luis agreed and soon began a Bible-teaching program so sound and systematic that he felt like he was attending a seminary. For three years, George Mereshian discipled Luis three hours a day, three days a week.

Luis began to devour commentaries and books by great Christians. When a particular passage struck him, Luis grabbed his pen and made a note in the margin. No matter how much he studied, he couldn't seem to quench his thirst for biblical truth.

One day Luis approached his supervisors at the bank. "Every day I've been completing my work in the foreign-operations department within a few hours. Would you mind if I spent the rest of my work time in personal study?"

Permission granted, Luis walked back to his desk, excited that he could study the Bible at work. Soon his coworkers began to call him "Pastor."

When Christmas arrived, the Palaus didn't bemoan the fact that they had nothing, literally, with which to celebrate. Instead of store-bought gifts, they made special gifts for each other. There were no parties or elaborate foods. But none of that mattered, because the family had so much fun singing and laughing together. Luis remembered how his father had shared Jesus with the neighbors at Christmastime and wanted to do the same. So he and his sisters walked to the city's nursing home to sing carols and tell the residents about Jesus Christ. They also went to Barranca, a nearby ghetto, armed with cookies, small gifts for the children, and the gospel.

One Sunday in church, the congregation sang the hymn, "Am I a Soldier of the Cross?" Enjoying the music, Luis belted out the words:

"Am I a soldier of the cross?
"A foll'wer of the Lamb?
"And shall I fear to own His cause
"Or blush to speak His name?"

Suddenly the lyrics by Isaac Watts became more than a catchy tune. It was as if God was saying to Luis: "You sing of being a soldier of the cross, and yet you do nothing. You have never suffered for Me; no one has ever said a thing to you against God. Think of Mildred Cable and Francesca French—those two missionary ladies from Asia."

Luis could hardly continue singing. He remembered his cowardly behavior back in Buenos Aires; he compared how little he was doing even now to the service of those inspiring women. *What kind of soldier are you?* he asked himself. *When were you ever dragged by the hair or stoned or spat upon for the gospel? You stand here and sing about being a soldier of the cross, but you are no soldier yet.*

Rebuked, Luis finally understood that all his Bible study and training at the church was a call from the Lord to serve Him and even suffer for Him, if necessary. "Will that service be as a banker?" Luis asked God. "A lawyer? A judge? I don't think so. I can't change my nation or the world through finances or law or politics or psychology. But no matter how I serve You, I'm going to have to become a soldier of the cross or quit singing about it."

Over the next several months, Luis struggled with his decision to choose God's will over his own. "I know You want all or nothing," Luis prayed. "You want me to be willing to do anything for You. I want to say 'yes' to You, God, but I'm afraid."

He stopped, picturing God sending him to Africa as a missionary to lepers. The white spots would be unnoticeable at first. Then they would grow bigger and bigger, covering his hands and face, then his entire body. Luis got up from his knees, shaking at the thought of contracting the dreaded disease. *I'll do anything for God,* Luis thought, *but not that.* Still, he agonized about his commitment to God's purpose.

Finally, kneeling by his bed one Saturday, Luis said, "Lord, yes, if it has to be, I'll even be a leper, for Your name's sake."

A few Sundays later, Luis was baptized at the church. As a baptismal day gift, his mother gave him a copy of C. H. Spurgeon's *Lectures to My Students,* a book on preaching and pastoral work. That night, Luis reread part of Spurgeon's book. *One day, I'll preach in Cordoba,* he thought. He fell asleep, dreaming about what God had in store for him in the days ahead.

That night, Luis suddenly sat up in bed, his heart racing. It was nearly midnight. *Am I really saved?* Luis asked himself. *Maybe I'm headed for hell.* Luis tried to calm his frantic thoughts, but his doubts continued. He ran to his mother's room and explained his fears. After listening to her wise and scriptural words, Luis cried out to the Lord in prayer. Only then did he regain a sense of His peace and assurance.

The experience showed Luis that Satan furiously objects when a Christian gives his life to God, and he can't resist attacking him to try and stamp him out. Luis could expect

Satan to try again.

After his baptism, Luis was permitted to help out with any church activity. He soon joined George Mereshian and others doing evangelistic street meetings. After several weeks of watching and learning, it was time for Luis to speak. He was nervous. Street meetings could fizzle fast if they weren't kept lively. Luis reviewed his notes as one of the group started singing and playing an instrument. A crowd gathered, and Luis started preaching, more worried about keeping people there than about whether he was saying everything just right. *I think I'm going to like this,* Luis said to himself after the meeting ended.

The group saw few conversions and encountered laughter, scorn, anger, and curiosity. Through it all, Luis learned one important principle: Christians have the truth. Christians stand on the truth. Let people argue and heckle all they want. Truth is truth, and any honest person who hears it knows it.

One day the elders asked Luis to speak at a youth meeting, which customarily was attended by the adults, as well. "You'll have several weeks to prepare," they said.

Luis began studying right away. On his knees, he read and reread Spurgeon's notes on Psalm 1 from *The Treasury of David.* He jotted down an outline. He prayed and prayed.

Finally, the big day—his first formal speaking engagement—arrived. Luis wondered if he could just not show up at church that day.

Instead, he walked into church on wooden legs and waited nervously for his turn, which arrived too soon for his comfort. Luis stood and faced the crowd of 120, including his beaming relatives.

God, I'm scared to death, he prayed silently. *Almost everyone in the audience knows as much or more about the Bible than I do. They expect a message from You. What if I don't say something exactly right? Oh, to be facing the crowds on a street corner!*

The congregation waited. Taking a deep breath, Luis began. With a dry throat and butterflies in his stomach, Luis read his notes aloud, rarely looking up from his scribbles. Less than twelve minutes later, he finished his sermon and sat down, feeling like a failure, but relieved that the ordeal was over.

Although Luis was growing spiritually, his finances seemed to shrink with each passing week. He worked hard at the bank and kept advancing, but the money never stretched very far.

Luis knew that God meant this situation for his good. Being poor was teaching him to look to God for everything. A bank strike during his second year in Cordoba cemented this truth in Luis's mind.

He hadn't been to work in forty-two days. With no income, he and his family had been forced to borrow money. Finally, the bank reopened and Luis was called back to work. But he didn't have the money for his eight- to ten-mile bus ride into town.

He got on his knees and prayed, "Lord, I'm going to trust You to take me to the bank without borrowing any more money." He knew just how God would answer his prayer. *I'll find a coin on the sidewalk just before the bus arrives.*

Early the next morning, Luis got ready for work and stepped into the dark, foggy outdoors. Arriving at the bus stop, he scanned the road for any sign of a coin. Nothing.

Undaunted, he headed toward the next bus stop, carefully looking for the elusive coin. *Someone easily could have dropped some money out of his pocket,* Luis thought. Still, nothing. *Well, there's another bus stop four blocks away. I'll check every inch of the street.*

By the time he reached the third stop, Luis felt discouraged. *You just have to have more faith, Palau,* he told himself. Empty-handed, Luis trudged past the fourth bus stop. *I'll just keep walking,* he thought. *Maybe the coin will be farther along.*

Just then, Luis saw a man trying to push an old car out of his garage. "Can I give you a hand?" Luis hollered.

"Sure," the man replied.

After getting the car out of the garage, the man jumped into the driver's seat. Luis pushed the car down the hill. With a jerk, the engine turned over and the man and car disappeared into the fog.

Luis began his own descent down the hill. About three blocks later, Luis heard a car idling beside him. The man Luis had helped moments earlier had returned. "I'm really embarrassed," he said. "You helped me push my car, and then I took off. Where are you going?"

"Right into the heart of town," Luis replied. "I work at the Bank of London."

The man smiled. "Hop in. I work at the bank across the street."

As Luis climbed into the car, he told himself, *Never again will I assume I know best how the Lord should answer my prayers.*

By the time Luis reached his early twenties, the elders had delegated more of the church work to him and several of the younger men. They held street meetings, spoke at little churches all over the countryside, sold Bibles, handed out tracts, visited the sick and elderly, organized a large Sunday school program, led youth meetings, and held all-night prayer meetings. They even developed a seven-minute daily radio program. The church was really hopping!

In the midst of their frenzied service for Christ, Luis and the others struggled to find a balance. An exhausted Luis asked himself again and again, *How do we rely on the indwelling Christ and not on our own efforts?*

After about two years, many of the committed men in the young people's group dropped out. "Why, Lord, why?" Luis asked God. "Why didn't they go the distance?" Frustrated, he wondered if he would ever fully experience the Holy Spirit's overflowing work.

Luis found it equally frustrating that his preaching had no power. He prepared and prayed, yet no one trusted Christ, except for a few children he had taught in vacation Bible school.

Nothing I do seems to make any difference, he thought. *It's obvious I don't have the gift that other evangelists have. I don't have the Holy Spirit's power in my life.*

Finally Luis gave God a deadline. "If I don't see any converts by the end of the year, I'm going to quit preaching. I'll still serve You; I'll still read and study and pray, but I won't do any more preaching."

The end of the year came and went. Luis's mind was made up—*I don't have the gift of evangelism.*

One Saturday morning, about four days into the new year, Luis pulled out his new copy of Billy Graham's *The Secret of Happiness,* shut the door so he wouldn't be distracted by his younger siblings and their friends, and curled up on the couch to read.

As despondent as he felt, Luis was encouraged by Billy Graham's thoughts on the Beatitudes from Jesus' Sermon on the Mount in Matthew 5. His study habits kicked into gear and he memorized the points Mr. Graham made on each Beatitude.

That night, Luis debated whether or not to attend home Bible study. Loyalty to the elders won out, and he boarded a bus for the short ride. As the evening commenced, the group sang several hymns, but the speaker never showed up.

Finally the man of the house said, "Luis, you're going to have to speak. None of the other preachers are here."

Remembering his promise, Luis tried to excuse himself, saying he wasn't prepared and had forgotten his Bible.

"Look, there's no one else, Luis. You have to speak."

With a quick prayer, Luis borrowed a New Testament and began. He read a Beatitude, repeated a few points he remembered from Billy Graham's book, read another verse, and so on.

Finally he came to the Beatitude, "Blessed are the pure in heart, for they shall see God" (Matthew 5:8 RSV). Suddenly, a woman from the neighborhood stood and began to cry. "Somebody help me! My heart is not pure. How am I going to find God?"

Luis turned the pages in his borrowed Bible and read, "The blood of Jesus, his Son, purifies us from all sin" (1 John 1:7). Before the evening was over, that woman found peace with God and went home with a pure heart overflowing with joy.

Luis ignored the buses that night and walked all the way home. "Thank You, God," Luis shouted into the starry night. "Thank You for choosing to use me!"

six

I don't remember that woman's name, Luis thought as the plane descended into Miami, *but I'll never forget her words:* "Somebody tell me how I can get a pure heart." He had delighted to lead her—and others who came in the months that followed—to Jesus Christ. The thrill of seeing that one soul enter the kingdom of heaven was just a taste of what God had in store for him during the next few years.

Luis could hardly believe the news—Billy Graham was evangelizing entire cities. He read reports of Mr. Graham's crusades in Los Angeles in 1949, in London in 1954. Thousands upon thousands were coming to Christ through his preaching.

That's the way to evangelize, he thought. *Sharing Christ with someone one-on-one is great; it's necessary. But eventually you must move the masses. A whole nation can*

52

be turned around by a small number of people trusting Christ. Mass evangelism—that's the key to revival, and, I'm convinced, that's where the Lord wants me.

He tore out a color picture of Mr. Graham from *Moody* magazine and pinned it on the wall near his bed.

"That's idolatry, Luis," his mother said.

"No, Mom," Luis replied, "I'm not worshiping him. He represents what God can do through a man." Silently, he added, *And it keeps alive my dream to share Jesus Christ with millions in Argentina and eventually all of Latin America.*

Luis shifted his studies into high gear. His search for knowledge was inspired by his desire to be the best evangelist possible. For nearly two years, he organized his day like school. He studied one subject for fifty minutes, took a ten-minute break, and turned to another subject, following this schedule for several hours. His heart felt like breaking when the time came to close his books and start work.

One day, Luis picked up a copy of *Time* magazine and read about a new invention called television. *God is going to use television to help evangelize the world,* he said to himself. *Someday my chance will come, and I'm going to make sure I'm ready for the Lord to use me for His glory.* On that day, and on many others, Luis stood in front of his mirror, pretending it was a television camera. He repeated to himself, "Look directly into the camera lens. That way each viewer will feel as though I'm talking directly to him. Don't get carried away with wild hand motions. Keep your gestures inside the range of the television camera." Then, staring at his reflection, he began to preach.

Taking a lesson from his mom, Luis spent hours each

week on his knees in prayer. One day, during this quiet time, he saw himself reaching out to great crowds of people, people by the thousands, stadiums full. *What's going on?* Luis asked himself. The mental picture seemed so real. At first, he attributed it to an overactive imagination. But in weeks to come, the image kept returning. *It must be from the Lord,* Luis decided. *He's laying on my heart what He's going to do. But it's going to take a miracle. There's no way I can accomplish something like that on my own.*

Luis resolved to continue to study and work and pray and preach and wait for God to move.

Meanwhile, he and his church friends, at the elders' encouragement, bought a tent and began holding meetings for people who wouldn't attend church. The group advertised for afternoon children's meetings and evening evangelistic rallies. People came, including many Christians who wanted to make the unsaved in the crowd feel more comfortable. Thrilled to be preaching the gospel, Luis spoke loudly and gestured expansively, as if he had a crowd of ten thousand.

"All I want, Lord, is to study, pray, preach, and lead more people to Christ," Luis prayed. "I can hardly wait for the day to come when I will be involved in a big crusade." That opportunity came sooner than he expected.

As general co-secretary of a national youth congress, Luis joined more than one thousand church leaders at a meeting with Jim Savage, a representative of the Billy Graham Evangelistic Association. He listened with excitement as Mr. Savage spoke about the possibility of Mr. Graham's coming to Argentina. Then the room darkened and Luis stared at the large projection screen down front. The image of Mr.

Graham appeared. Luis's eyes widened as he saw the tens of thousands of Christian leaders in India to whom Mr. Graham was speaking.

It's almost like he's here in the room with me, Luis thought as the camera zoomed in on Mr. Graham's face. He was preaching from Ephesians 5:18, "And do not be drunk with wine, in which is dissipation; but be filled with the Spirit" (NKJV). The crowd in India no longer existed for Luis. Mr. Graham was looking right at him and shouting, "Are you filled with the Spirit? Are you filled with the Spirit? Are you filled with the Spirit?"

At that moment, Luis realized, *That's my problem. That's what causes my up-and-down Christianity. That's why I have zeal and commitment but little fruit or victory. I don't know how to be filled with all the fullness of God Himself.*

Back home, Luis began receiving more and more requests to speak at different meetings. "Luis," his mother said, "God has given you a gift; He has given you a heart for evangelism. I think you should leave your job at the bank and spend all your time in ministry."

"Mom, how are you going to live?" Luis objected. "We have a lot of mouths to feed!"

"Luis, you know if the Lord is in it, He will provide."

"But I don't feel the call," Luis said. "I don't have that final call that tells me it would be all right."

"The call? What call?" she said. "He gave the commission two thousand years ago, and you've read it all your life. How many times do you want Him to give the commandment before you obey it? It isn't a question of call; it's a question of obedience. The call He has given; it's the answer He's waiting for."

Luis turned away. He knew his mother was right, but he didn't have enough confidence in the Lord to quit his job just yet.

One day, in late 1958, Luis received a flier announcing a meeting with two American speakers: Dick Hillis, a former missionary to China and president of Overseas Crusades International (OC), and Ray Stedman, a pastor from Palo Alto, California.

What does a pastor from California look like? Luis wondered. *I guess I'll have to go and find out.* After the meeting, Luis noticed Ray Stedman standing alone. He walked up to him and said, in English, "Hi. I'm Luis."

The conversation started rolling. Encouraged by all the questions Ray was asking, Luis told him all about himself, his job, his motorbike, and his family.

"Luis, how about coming to a Bible study tomorrow morning?" Ray asked. "It's a small gathering—me and a few other missionaries."

Flattered, Luis agreed.

The next day, after the Bible study, Ray mentioned that he needed to do some shopping. "I can give you a ride on my motorbike," Luis said. As the two shopped together, they continued their conversation. It wasn't long before Ray asked, "Luis, would you like to go to seminary?"

"It would be nice," Luis replied, "but I'm not sure I'll ever make it. I don't have a lot of money, and my church doesn't encourage formal theological education."

"Well," Ray contintued, "it could be arranged if the Lord wanted it. How would you like to come to the United States?"

"I've thought about it. Maybe someday I'll be able to go, the Lord willing." Then Luis added silently, *But I doubt the Lord will ever bring that "someday" to pass.*

"You know, Luis," Ray responded, "the Lord may just will it."

The next night, after hearing Dick Hillis speak, Luis went with the two Americans to the airport. "I'll see you in the United States," Ray said.

"Well, the Lord willing, maybe someday," Luis said.

"No, Luis, the Lord *is* going to will. I'll write you from the plane."

All the way home, Luis thought about Ray Stedman. *He's a nice man. A bit unrealistic, though. If he makes as little money as the ministers in South America, it will take ten years before he has saved enough to get me to the United States. So why even dream?*

When Luis checked the mail a few days later, he saw an envelope addressed to him from Ray Stedman. Luis ripped it open and began to read the exciting news. Ray knew a businessman who wanted to finance Luis's trip to the United States so he could study at Dallas Theological Seminary.

"Wow!" Luis exclaimed. "Attending Dallas would be wonderful." Almost immediately, however, Luis's excitement cooled. He grabbed a pen and paper and began to write:

"Thanks for the offer, but there's too much to do. Too many people are going to hell for me to be spending four more years reading books. I can study at home. I'm disciplined, and I enjoy studying. No, I'm needed here. Besides, who else will take care of my family?"

Luis soon received another letter from Ray. "You don't need to worry about your family, Luis," he wrote. "Someone from the United States will provide for them, too."

Luis didn't know how to respond to Ray's incredible

offer, so he didn't. *I'm so busy right now; I don't have time to write another letter,* Luis thought, trying to soothe his conscience. Days turned into weeks. Luis received another letter from Ray, then another. He read them, then tossed them aside without responding. *God is opening so many doors for ministry and evangelism here. And then there's the decision I have to make about my job at the bank.*

A few days later, Luis confronted the bank manager, even though he realized it might cost him his job. "Sir, recently you've implemented a few new policies that make me uncomfortable," Luis began. "I know these practices aren't illegal. But they raise some ethical questions for me. You may know I'm a Christian, and I'm not sure I now can do everything that's required of my job."

Angrily, the manager reminded Luis of all the bank had done for him and all they had planned for him. "Palau, I wouldn't rock the boat if I were you," he said, then dismissed Luis with a wave of his hand.

Luis slowly walked down the hall. *It won't be long before the home office in Buenos Aires hears about this incident,* Luis thought. *I bet the manager already has started his report. I could be fired tomorrow.*

Four days later, Luis noticed an American opening a new account. He greeted the man in English, and they started talking. He was Keith Bentson, representing SEPAL (Servicio Evangelizador Para América Latina), the Latin American division of OC. "I'm a Christian, too," Luis told him. "I've even met OC's leader, Dick Hillis. He was here in Cordoba not long ago."

A few days later, Keith returned to make his first deposit. He told Luis, "I'm looking for a bilingual Christian man who might want to work for SEPAL. The job is translating English material into Spanish for our magazine, *La Voz* (The Voice)."

"You've got your man," Luis said.

"Who?" Keith asked.

"It's me."

"Oh, Luis, you'd better think about it and talk with your family. We're talking about a very, very small salary; no doubt much less than you're making here."

"I'll talk to my family," Luis promised, "but I'm your man. This is exciting. I'm sure it's of God."

With his mother's blessing, Luis gave the bank his final notice. Even the shock of the very tiny salary didn't deter him. He had finally found a way to get into full-time Christian work.

Moving from number four man at the bank to low man at SEPAL didn't bother Luis one bit. He loved his new job and the variety of work—doing everything from translation to representing the mission at conventions. And he still could continue with his tent meetings.

One Wednesday, a few weeks into his job, Keith said, "Luis, if you're willing, I would like you to stay at the office after closing time. I'd like to pray with you."

Keith prayed for Luis and his family, then the Brethren church they attended and all the elders, naming each one. *How can he know all that information?* Luis asked himself. *He doesn't even attend my church.* Inspired by Keith's passionate prayer, Luis prayed, too.

The next Wednesday, Keith invited Luis to stay again. This time, he brought a map of the city of Cordoba and pinpointed the fifteen or sixteen local churches of the Brethren movement. When Keith began praying, he again named each church and its leaders. "Oh, God," he implored as he paced the room, "bless these men for Your service and Your glory!"

By the end of their prayer time, Luis felt as if he had taken a trip around the city on his knees. *So this is what intercessory prayer is all about,* Luis thought. *How thrilling!*

By the next Wednesday, Keith's map of the city included churches of all denominations. He prayed for each one, again knowing the pastor's name, in most cases. Back and forth they prayed. First Keith, then Luis, then Keith again.

Luis told Keith one day, "I've always wondered why, when I was taught about unity in Christ, that oneness shouldn't include devout Christians of other denominations. You've helped me understand the meaning of Ephesians 6:18, where we're told to pray for all the saints."

As the weeks went by, Keith's map got bigger, and Luis's vision grew. First, Argentina, then the continent of South America, then other nations and continents, until finally they had prayed for the whole world. *No matter where they live, they all need Jesus,* Luis said to himself. *All people everywhere need Jesus Christ.*

When he wasn't busy at SEPAL, Luis and his friends would set up the tent for yet another evangelistic rally. "If only we had an actual team of talented men and women," Luis said over and over again. "Two or three people who can travel around with us to lead singing or play music, instead of my sister playing an accordion. But we don't have the money, and I don't even know where to begin to look."

One night after the tent meeting, a young American walked up to Luis. "My name is Bruce Woodman," he said. "I'm a missionary here, and I've been looking for a ministry to get involved in. If you need a soloist and song leader for your meetings, I would love to help out.

"I also know a keyboard man, Bill Fasig," Bruce continued. "He used to work under New York evangelist Jack Wyrtzen. Are you interested in us?"

"Yes. Yes I am," Luis replied. "You are an answer to my prayers."

At the next tent meeting, Luis watched Bruce and Bill work. *Bruce is the perfect emcee, song leader, and soloist,* Luis thought. *He really gets the crowd excited. And Bill's music makes a noticeable difference. We've just graduated. Now we have a team.*

One day, Luis received another letter from Ray. "Your inaction is irresponsible and rude," he rebuked Luis. "I've invited you to the United States at no cost. If you want to come, come. You won't be forced to attend Dallas Theological Seminary or stay anywhere else for four years."

Then Ray described an alternative to four years in seminary:

"You might want to look into a one-year graduate course in theology available at Multnomah Biblical Seminary in Portland, Oregon. You said you wanted the opportunity to ask questions of Bible teachers and get answers to those tough ones you haven't been able to resolve through your own reading. Multnomah might suit your needs. What's more, you can spend a few months before and after the school year as an intern at my church in California, together with another young man, Dallas Theological Seminary student Charles Swindoll."

Luis got the point. If he had kept the lines of communication open, any questions he had would have been answered and the obstacles he imagined would have been swept aside.

Then Luis saw the check that Ray had sent to help his

mother during his absence and to pay for his trip to Buenos Aires.

"God," he prayed, "I have no more excuses. I've felt for a long time that You might want me to go to the United States to see more of the world and broaden my understanding. Now the door is wide open. I'm going to go."

Luis told the people at his church and at SEPAL about his decision. "Why don't you reconsider, Luis?" they told him. "If you go, you might never return to South America. Your ministry is down here; this is God's will for you, in spite of how attractive the States are."

But Luis knew, despite their objections, that in a few months he would board the plane for the States.

Luis also knew that his girlfriend felt uneasy about his decision. He had his own doubts—but his were about their relationship. *Everyone thinks we should get married,* Luis said to himself. *But I'm just not ready. True, I'm twenty-four and I think I'm mature enough. But I have no savings. And I still get so upset when things go wrong. I wonder, sometimes, if she's the girl God has for me. I don't want to hurt her, though. Maybe going to the States will get me out of this relationship.*

While at the office one day, Luis heard someone call his name. "Hey, Luis, come here. You've got to hear the plan Ed has come up with."

Luis hurried over to the small group of Americans: Keith Bentson, Bruce Woodman, and Ed Murphy—one of SEPAL's most energetic new missionaries.

Ed explained again how they could take a group of excited national believers from a nearby town into a place void of any Christian witness, hold evangelistic meetings, disciple the new converts, and leave behind an active, functioning

New Testament church—all within a few days.

"I want in," Luis told the group.

Later Luis told his mother, "We've chosen Oncativo, a town of about twelve thousand people, as our target. It appears to be totally pagan. Our 'scout' asked around, and only one person could recall having ever seen an evangelical Christian or held a tract in his hand—and that was forty years earlier!"

A few weeks before he left for the States, Luis, the three Americans, and five church members from Rio Segundo, a nearby town, arrived in Oncativo. The nine men approached one of the town's councilmen and asked if they could speak to the people during the national celebration the next day.

"No," he replied bluntly.

"Then may our musicians join the parade and play some national songs?" they asked.

Again he said, "No."

As they walked away, the group talked among themselves. "This is great! We stood strong for God and the gospel in the midst of opposition. We made bold requests. Let's keep trying."

Next they went to a print shop in town that was owned by a Swiss family. They explained why they were in the city, and the shop owner finally agreed to let Luis and the team use their storage room off the print shop for evangelistic meetings.

The gracious family invited the nine men to eat dinner with them. During the meal, they once again shared their mission, not knowing that the Spirit of God was working in the heart of the middle-aged, unmarried daughter of the house. Right at the dinner table, she received Christ, becoming the first convert that week.

Early the next morning, Luis and the men walked around the city, knocking on doors and handing out hundreds of fliers announcing their meetings. Then they hurried back to the park where they began to play march tunes and patriotic songs. A crowd gathered, then Luis stood up, preached a brief message, and invited everyone to attend that night's meeting. Finally they headed back to the little storage room. Seventy-five people could fit in that room; they were going to pray that a good portion of their meeting hall would be filled.

That evening, Luis watched the townspeople pack the place. He could hardly wait to begin preaching. The passage he had chosen was one of his favorites, John 10:28–29. In it, Jesus gave these word of assurance:

"I give them eternal life, and they shall never
perish; no one can snatch them out of my hand.
My Father, who has given them to me, is greater
than all; no one can snatch them out of my
Father's hand."

As he preached, Luis thought about the decision he had made earlier during prayer. *At the end of my message, I'm going to invite people to publicly confess Jesus Christ— something I've never done before. The church elders always discouraged me from using such an "emotional technique." But I feel God wants me to give a public invitation. I will be disobeying the Lord if I ignore His prompting.*

Finally the time arrived. Luis asked everyone who wanted to receive Christ to bow their heads and pray along with him. Then he said, "All those who prayed with me, please raise your hands to signify your decision."

Almost three dozen hands flew up.

So the critics are right! Luis thought, almost in a panic. *It is all emotion. These invitations are unfair. The people feel pressured; their emotions have been tampered with.*

"Please, lower your hands," he said. "Let me explain again." Then he spent another half hour on the passage, clarifying each point, making sure those listening understood what was meant by choosing life with Christ. Another prayer, and Luis again asked for hands. Even more went up!

By the end of the week of meetings, a church had been planted. Seventy people had trusted Jesus Christ as their Savior; and they received instruction about baptism, Communion, witnessing, music, being elders, and preaching the Word—everything Luis and the others could fit into that short time. The team members from the neighboring town of Rio Segundo would be watching over the new church, which eventually planted several churches in other nearby towns.

Home again, Luis began packing for his trip to the United States. In a few days, he would be on his way.

seven

Luis climbed off the plane and walked into the terminal at Miami Airport. He had said a tearful farewell to his friends and family at the Ezeiza International Airport in Buenos Aires, and his final destination was still half a continent away—Ray Stedman's church in Palo Alto, California.

"If I ever make it there," Luis said aloud. "First, I have to find a connecting flight to replace the one I missed." Bleary-eyed, he looked down at his rumpled black suit. The ten extra hours on the plane hadn't done it or him any good.

What would my friends think of me now? Luis thought, then chuckled to himself. He laughed again as he replayed in his mind his mother's last-minute advice: "Don't go into the cities, don't travel alone, watch out, don't get shot and stuffed into a trunk, and remember Hebrews 13:5 and 6!"

"Sorry, Mom. I'm going to have to break one of your rules," Luis said as he hailed a cab. Minutes later, he arrived at the house of some Cuban friends of his brother- in-law.

After a collect call to Ray Stedman—"Yes, I'm still planning to speak at church when I arrive Sunday evening"—and a restless attempt at getting a few hours of sleep, Luis boarded a Delta jet bound for San Francisco. He stared as the flight attendants gave away free cups of coffee, sugar, plastic spoons, maps, and postcards. *I must be in the land of opportunity,* Luis said to himself. *Now this is living!*

From his window, Luis watched as the jet flew over the big cities of the United States and finally descended into San Francisco. He began to think, *Someday we'll have evangelistic crusades in the U.S. It doesn't matter that I have never seen a crusade. I know from my experience in Oncativo, from everything I have read, and from the burden God has put on my heart that it is only a matter of time.*

Luis walked into the airport and searched in vain for Ray Stedman's familiar face. A woman's voice at his shoulder made him turn. "Luis, I'm Elaine, Ray's wife." Listening to her reassuring words of greeting, Luis tried to smile. *Everything here is so foreign,* Luis thought wearily. *Even my suit looks out of place. Maybe America isn't the place for me. Maybe I should go home.* Instead, clutching a single suitcase, Luis followed Elaine to her car.

"Sunday evening service is about to begin," she explained as she merged into the Bayshore Freeway traffic and raced the twenty-five miles to Peninsula Bible Church in Palo Alto. They rushed into church several minutes late. At Elaine's encouragement, Luis marched right down the aisle and onto the platform next to Ray. Later that night, as he recalled the accompanying applause, Luis knew he had never before received such a warm welcome.

Homesick at first, Luis became fast friends with the

Stedmans and their four daughters. He enjoyed the father–son relationship that he was developing with Ray, listening carefully to his advice, counsel, and even reprimands. Ray even began calling Luis "my son" when he introduced him.

That summer, a government official from India visited the church. After listening to the man speak, Luis approached him and asked, "What's the best technique for getting near people in power? What method do you use on presidents or other government leaders?"

The official put his arm around Luis and smiled. "Young man," he said, "there are no techniques. You must just love them."

Walking away, Luis thought, *He's putting me on. He has some great secret that he's not willing to share with me.* Little did Luis know that these words would be the wisest counsel he would ever receive.

His two months with the Stedmans passed too quickly. Luis still had a lot to learn about American culture—how to chat and eat and behave the way the natives did. Now his lessons would come from the students and teachers he would meet up north at Multnomah Biblical Seminary in Portland, Oregon.

Luis received royal treatment from his fellow students at Multnomah. He made a lot of friends and began to teach Sunday school and speak in area churches. Occasionally, he was asked to speak at Multnomah's daily chapel service. He studied hard, and found the first semester courses on biblical anthropology and the doctrine of the indwelling Christ especially demanding.

"I'm still struggling, God," Luis prayed one day. "I want more fruit in my personal life. I want to be able to live out the lifestyle I see in men like Ray Stedman, who over-flow with joy and release and freedom. But how, God? The more I try, the more such a lifestyle eludes me. If I didn't care so much about serving You and preaching the gospel, I think I would give up and go back to Cordoba."

No one at Multnomah would have guessed that this friendly, winsome, somewhat different Latin American was fighting such spiritual battles. All Luis wanted was to become the person everyone thought he was.

When Thanksgiving arrived, Luis felt anything but thank-ful. He needed cash—and quick. If he was going to con-tinue seminary, he had to pay his bill for the next semester, which would begin in about a month. No one but God knew about his financial difficulties. He hadn't mentioned or even hinted to anyone that he needed money. "Besides," Luis said aloud, "who would I ask? Why should anyone give me ten dollars, let alone pay for another half a year of seminary?"

The more he thought about his situation, the more depressed he became. *God has given up on me,* Luis decided. *As soon as the term is over, I'm going back to Argentina.*

That weekend, Luis checked his campus mailbox. "Great," he said, as he pulled out a plain envelope with his name on it. "Not even a letter from home. Nothing but a graded paper."

Luis opened the envelope and pulled out a note typed on plain white paper. He looked for a signature, but found none. He had no way to tell who it was from. He began to read:

> *Dear Luis,*
> *You have been a great blessing to many of us*

69

*here in the States, and we appreciate what you
have taught us. We feel that you deserve help to
finish your year at Multnomah; therefore, all your
tuition and books have been paid for.*

*Just check in at the business office, and they
will finalize the papers. So you will be grateful to
every American you have met or will ever meet,
we remain anonymous.*

So God is still with me after all! Luis thought. *I may
feel defeated and frustrated, but God wants me to know He
is there and to hang in and stay at seminary.*

One evening a few weeks before the semester ended,
Luis headed over to a class party along with several other
people. Unsure why, he approached a young woman named
Patricia Scofield and said, "Can I walk you over?"

"Sure," she said.

At the party, they went their separate ways, but Luis
was now interested in the tall, thin, sandy-haired school-
teacher from Portland. In class, Luis realized how smart
and mature she appeared. As he ate in the dining hall, he
noticed how well she dressed. Then, as he talked with her,
he discovered how spiritually sensitive she seemed.

"I want to become a missionary," Pat told him one day.
"I spent a year teaching in the Portland public schools. But
after I complete my year of required Bible training, I plan
on joining OC to teach missionary children in Taiwan."

Luis was smitten. In the morning, he would look out
his window, which overlooked the walkway to the cafete-
ria. When he saw Pat, he ran to the door and popped out
just in time to escort her to breakfast.

When he learned that Pat usually studied in the library,

he could be found there, too—one eye on his book, the other eye on her.

Pat finally caught on that Luis was interested, and the two saw a lot of each other. *There may be nothing serious between us yet,* Luis thought, *but I certainly hope there will be.*

When Luis learned that Pat was going away over the Christmas break and had a few stops to make, he began to worry. *What if one of those stops is to see an old boyfriend?* he asked himself. *I have to let her know how I feel.* As soon as he could, he pulled Pat aside; he didn't have time for dramatics or romance. Looking her straight in the eye, Luis said, "Pat, you are a special person and have become very special to me." He paused, halfway expecting Pat to break in to stop him. Encouraged by her silence, Luis continued, "I care for you a great deal. I hope we can spend a lot more time together after the holidays."

A few days later, Luis walked glumly into Mult- nomah's chapel. This would be one of the last chapel ser- vices before he and Pat went their separate ways for Christmas break. Attendance at chapel was required, and lately Luis had taken to sitting in the back. Looking straight at the speaker, Luis would dare him to make him pay attention. *If he's good, I'll listen,* Luis told himself. *If not, I'll review my class notes.*

On this particular day, the speaker was Major Ian Thomas, founder and general director of the Torchbearers, the group that ran the Capernwray Hall Bible School in England.

Major Thomas's thick British accent and staccato deliv- ery immediately hooked Luis. But what really intrigued him was when Major Thomas pointed a finger that had been par- tially cut off.

71

Now here's an interesting man, Luis thought. And in twenty-two minutes, Ian Thomas got through to him.

"It took Moses forty years in the wilderness to realize that he was nothing," Major Thomas said. "God was trying to tell Moses, 'I don't need a pretty bush or an educated bush or an eloquent bush. Any old bush will do, as long as I am in the bush. If I am going to use you, I am going to use you. It will not be you doing something for Me, but Me doing something through you.'

"The burning bush in the desert was likely a dry bunch of ugly little sticks that had hardly developed, yet Moses had to take off his shoes. Why? Because this was holy ground. Why? Because God was in the bush!"

That's it, Luis felt like yelling. *I'm that kind of bush: a worthless, useless bunch of dried-up old sticks. I can do nothing for God. All my reading and studying and asking questions and trying to model myself after others is worthless. Everything in my ministry is worthless, unless God is in the bush. Only He can make something happen. Only He can make it work.*

Major Thomas then told of many Christian workers who failed at first because they thought they had something to offer God. He said, "I myself once imagined that because I was an aggressive, winsome, evangelistic sort, God could use me. But God didn't use me until I came to the end of myself."

Luis thought, *That's exactly my situation. I am at the end of myself.*

Then Major Thomas concluded with Galatians 2:20:

" 'I have been crucified with Christ; it is no longer I who live, but Christ who lives in me; and the life I now live in the flesh I live by faith in the Son of God, who loved me and gave himself for me' " (RSV).

Luis ran back to his room in tears and fell to his knees next to his bunk. He prayed in Spanish, "Lord, now I get it. I understand. I see the light at the end of the tunnel. The whole thing is 'not I, but Christ in me.' It's not what I'm going to do for You but rather what You're going to do through me."

For the next hour and a half, Luis stayed on his knees, communing with the Lord in prayer. "I finally realize that the reason I hated myself inside is because I wrongly loved myself outside. Please forgive my pride in thinking I was something special because of my jobs and my ministries and my relationships with Christian leaders. I thought I was really something, but You weren't active in the bush. I never gave You a chance.

"I don't want to place my confidence in the opportunities. Instead, make me grateful for all the small things You have put in my life to make me a better preacher. I want to depend not on myself or my breaks, but on Christ alone— the indwelling, resurrected, almighty Lord Jesus."

Luis knew this day marked the intellectual turning point in his spiritual life. He could hardly contain his excitement. *I can relax and rest in Jesus,* he thought. *I feel such peace knowing I can quit struggling.*

eight

Luis could hardly wait to return to Multnomah for his
second semester. Spending time with the Stedmans
was great, but he missed Pat. A bit guiltily, he thought
about the girl back home he had been dating. *She's a nice,
cultured, educated girl from a wonderful churchgoing family. Everyone thinks we should be married. At first I
thought so, too. But I've known for a long time now we
weren't meant to be together. I don't want to hurt her,
though.*

"What's up, Luis?" Ray Stedman asked, interrupting
his thoughts.

Luis told him about Pat and his feelings for her.

"What about that girl from South America? Have you
told her about Pat? Have you written her and told her it's
over?"

"I haven't even written my mother in a long time," Luis
said, "but I'll get to it."

Throughout the summer, Ray kept mentioning the letter, and Luis kept promising to write it.

Finally, Ray sat Luis down. "Look, Luis," he said, "you've really got to write."

"Don't worry; I'll write," Luis said, then added silently, *when I'm good and ready.*

But Ray would not be put off that easily. "It's going to cause a lot of hurt. The longer you prolong the relationship, the more bad feelings you'll cause. You could leave a trail of hurt people if you aren't careful. It's not good, and it's not right."

"When I get back down there, I'll clear it up," Luis said. "I'll have a little chat with them, and it'll be all over." He watched Ray's eyes grow cold. He knew he had gone too far.

"You know, my son," Ray said, putting his arm around Luis, "you really think you can solve any problem with that mouth."

Luis opened his mouth to object, but Ray continued. "Listen to me, Luis. One of these days you are going to dig a hole so deep with your mouth that not even God will be able to pull you out of it—unless you shape up."

"I didn't mean it that way," Luis replied weakly.

"Oh, but you did mean it that way, Luis. You said you would solve everything with a little chat, and that's exactly what you meant. You are so self-confident that it oozes from your pores. Well, God can't stand self-confident people, and He'll not use you until you are selfless. You'll be nothing; you'll go nowhere."

Although the words hurt, Luis knew they were the truth. Ray loved him too much to let him get away with that behavior. A few days later, after the shock wore off,

Luis wrote his letter. "I'll never forget the counsel I received from Ray," he later said. "It was chastisement from the Lord, and I needed it."

His second semester at Multnomah was exciting, and he did exceptionally well in all his classes—except for the course on the New Testament Book of Hebrews. He gave partial credit for the one C he received to Pat. His studies, although important, paled next to the thought of spending time with her. The two saw each other as often as they could.

On Valentine's Day, Luis and Pat went out for the evening. The rain, typical of February in Portland, didn't stop the two from going for a long walk. Holding the umbrella, Luis turned to Pat and asked, "Will you return to South America with me?" He hoped she understood his intentions.

"Yes, Luis, I will," Pat replied.

The two were unofficially engaged. A few days later, a quick meeting with the president of Multnomah made the engagement official.

Pat soon noticed that Luis seemed reluctant to discuss their upcoming marriage. She decided to broach the topic. "Luis, my dad has been figuring out how to pay for our wedding."

"Pay for the wedding?" Luis repeated. "What does that mean?"

"It's the custom here that the parents of the bride pay for the wedding," Pat replied.

"Everything?" Luis asked, his voice raising in excitement.

"Of course—except for the rehearsal dinner, and we can go simple on that."

"That's great news!" Luis said, his relief evident on his

face. He then thought, *I'm glad Americans have different customs. In Argentina, we would have to split the expenses, and there is no way my mother and sisters could afford to pay for anything wedding related. I love America!*

At the end of the school year, Pat remained in Portland, while Luis headed back to Palo Alto to continue his internship with Ray Stedman at Peninsula Bible Church.

For two long months, the couple communicated by mail. Phone calls cost money—something neither of them had. In one letter, Luis wrote to Pat about his conversation with one of the church elders, Bob Connell:

"You have to remember, Pat, that the pastors and elders of Peninsula Bible Church don't go around making predictions about the future. Besides, I've never told anyone except you about my dreams to become an evangelist and speak at crusades around the world. Who would take me seriously, especially since I still haven't even seen an evangelistic crusade?

"The other day, though, Bob pulled me aside and said, 'Luis, I believe God's going to use you to win as many souls as Billy Graham—even in this country.' I didn't know what to say. But in my heart I feel God's going to do this. Pat, I know that day will come."

After completing his internship, Luis loaded up his old '55 Buick he had bought from the Stedmans and raced back up the coast, arriving in Portland a few days before the wedding.

On August 5, 1961, Luis and Pat became husband and wife in a marriage ceremony jointly officiated by Ray Stedman and their pastor in Portland, Albert Wollen.

Their two-week honeymoon ended with a drive down to the San Francisco Bay Area, where they were interviewed

77

by the OC board. Being accepted for missionary service in Colombia meant they had to hustle back to Portland and pack for their missionary internship in Detroit.

As they traveled across the country, Luis and Pat talked for hours on end and visited the usual tourist sites, all of them brand-new to Luis. Pat soon learned about her husband's quick temper when his best-foot-forward courting approach gave way to the real Luis Palau.

Soon they arrived in Detroit, their home for seven months. The internship program was tougher than either of them had expected. The woman the Palaus lived with refused to put a lock on their bedroom door and would burst in at inopportune times. And the church they served worked them hard, but neglected them financially.

"I can't believe these people," Luis told Pat one day. "The freewill offering we received this week consists of twenty-five cents and a few cans of food someone didn't want. We're supposed to live off of that? I thought I could handle just about anything, but this is too much."

So off Luis went to see Fred Renich, director of the internship program. Assuming Fred knew exactly what was going on, Luis blew his stack. He ranted and raved for several minutes about the bad treatment they were receiving. Then Luis said, "I've had it up to here. We want to leave."

"You don't have to go home," Mr. Renich said. "We're going to rectify the situation and move you next week. But first I want to tell you something. You know how to go to just the right person to get action, and in the process you don't stop to think of how many people you step on, or how many people you may even destroy. You don't care about that because all you care about is action.

"The problem," he continued, "is that you have a quiet

78

wife. If you don't learn to put that choleric temperament under the control of Jesus Christ, you're going to walk all over Pat, and she just may not let you know. Then one day you'll have destroyed her, and you won't even realize it."

Walk all over Pat? Luis said to himself, stunned. *But I love her.*

"Think back on your life," Mr. Renich urged Luis. "Go back to your room and think about all the people you've hurt, all the people you've stepped on, and perhaps all the spiritual corpses on the side of the road you traveled to get where you are today. List their names, and then do whatever it takes to make things right."

In earnest, Luis began making his list. He had more than a few old friends and acquaintances to contact and apologize to for past actions.

During the summer of 1962, the Palaus returned to Palo Alto for three weeks of orientation with OC. Normally, after orientation, new missionaries immediately begin deputation work to raise the money they need to go overseas. But because Luis expected to be heavily involved in evangelistic crusades someday, OC sent the Palaus to Fresno to serve as volunteers for Billy Graham's crusade in July.

Luis began visiting Spanish churches to encourage them to participate, while Pat helped arrange for the large groups that would come by bus or train. During the crusade itself, she was to work at the counseling table, and he was to interpret for the Spanish audience.

Throughout those weeks of preparation for the crusade, Luis didn't miss a thing. He asked questions nonstop and recorded every detail in a thick notebook. He wanted to be ready for the day when he would organize a crusade.

At a pre-crusade breakfast, the Palaus finally got to

meet Billy Graham. "Stay with the big cities," Mr. Graham told Luis when he learned that Luis dreamed of preaching at evangelistic crusades. "Paul always went to the centers of population. And Mr. Moody used to say that the cities were the mountains, and if you won the mountains, the valleys took care of themselves."

With the end of the crusade, the Palaus began deputation work. For the rest of the summer, they traveled up and down the coast, visiting churches that might help support their work with Ed Murphy in Colombia.

One day, Luis received the news that he needed to report to San Francisco to be sworn in as a citizen. Not long after his marriage, Luis had filled out the paperwork and passed the examination on U.S. history and government. He wanted to make America his home.

The day finally arrived. Luis stood before a United States judge and proudly repeated the oath of allegiance: "I hereby declare, on oath, that I absolutely and entirely renounce and abjure all allegiance and fidelity to any foreign prince, potentate, state or sovereignty. . . ."

Immediately after the ceremony, Luis climbed into his old Buick and drove to a bridge along the old Bayshore Freeway. He parked his car and looked again at his certificate of American citizenship. "Signed by the Kennedy brothers," he said. "John F. Kennedy, president of the United States, and Robert Kennedy, the U.S. attorney general." Luis climbed out of the car, his green card in his hand. *As a citizen, I no longer need this document,* Luis thought. *I don't need a permission slip to live and work in America.* As he walked over to the railing of the bridge, he began ripping the card. Finally, leaning out as far as he dared, Luis ceremoniously tossed the pieces over the side.

As they fluttered into the bay, Luis shouted, "I am now an American!"

Luis couldn't be happier. He had become a citizen and soon he would become a father.

nine

Luis, it's time," Pat announced. "I need to go to the hospital."

"What?" Luis said in shock. "It's January. You're only seven months along. We were going to finish our deputation work here in California and return to Portland before the baby arrives. You can't have it now!"

Pat said, "Tell that to the baby," and off they went to Stanford University Hospital.

Luis sat in the hallway, waiting for information. He had been waiting for more than an hour when he saw the doctor, a Christian friend from Palo Alto, walking toward him.

"Luis," he said, "there are serious complications."

"What's wrong?"

"I'm not sure yet, Luis. We just have to pray."

Luis was scared to death. He tried to sit, but couldn't. He began to pace the hallway as he prayed for Pat and their baby. At every turn, he peeked down the hallway, trying to see the doctor, looking for any sign of news.

Another hour passed. The doctor still hadn't come out, and Luis feared the worst. When the doctor finally appeared, he looked more worried than ever. "We're getting an incredibly strong heartbeat for only a seven-month fetus," he said, "and it is so irregular that I must tell you I'm not optimistic. I don't know how the baby is surviving with the heartbeat we're hearing."

Luis felt close to tears. Two more hours passed with Luis in constant prayer. *We must have lost the baby,* Luis said to himself. *Otherwise, the doctor would have come back by now.* Then he looked up and saw the obstetrician walking swiftly toward him.

"Congratulations!" the doctor said, with a huge grin. "You're the father of twin boys! What we heard were two regular heartbeats."

Luis literally jumped for joy.

Because Kevin and Keith were premature, weighing less than four pounds each, they had to stay in the hospital for five weeks. "I just want to hold them," Luis kept saying. Finally, the day arrived when the Palaus brought their two boys home—healthy and strong.

Later that year, the Palaus flew to Costa Rica. They arrived only a few days before Christmas. The Spanish Language Institute in which Pat was enrolled began in January 1964.

Pat attempted to brighten the drab apartment for the holidays, but the only decorations she had were the Christmas stockings her mother had made. The search for a Christmas tree proved futile. Besides being too expensive to purchase, the trees in the shops had been cut as early as September in Canada. Loud Latin music that Pat couldn't understand replaced the traditional carols she was used to hearing. The extreme heat made baking holiday treats impossible. Besides, Pat had all she could handle trying to keep the gritty ash billowing from the Volcano Irazu out of her home and the hands of her two crawling boys.

On Christmas eve, Pat began to cry.

"What's wrong?" Luis asked.

"I just wish we were back in the States right now. I've tried to make adjustments, but there are just so many. I've never been outside the United States. My family seems so far away. And tomorrow we'll celebrate Christmas in a way so foreign that it might as well be the seventh of February."

Luis tried to comfort Pat, but what brightened her spirits was a visit the next day from David and Betty Constance, a couple from the language school. Their lighthearted fun, along with the roasted chicken dinner they brought, helped make that untraditional Christmas into a memorable one.

With the holidays behind them, the Palaus began to search earnestly for a housekeeper. Someone was needed to tend the twins while Pat attended school. No one could be found. So on the first day of classes, Luis became Mr. Mom. *How hard can it be?* he asked himself as he said good-bye to Pat. *I may have grown up in a culture where men do not handle the babies except to hug and kiss them. But I watched my sisters Matilde and Martha take care of our younger siblings. There's nothing to it.*

After a couple of days, Luis couldn't take it any longer. Impatiently, he told the Lord, "Is this what I came here for? I left my country to go to seminary. I've been through missionary internship. I've completed deputation. And now here I am on the mission field. But instead of preaching and winning souls, I'm stuck at home, day after day. . . burping babies and changing messy diapers!"

Then he received a gentle reminder from the Lord: *"Just a minute, Luis. You are always reminding people that they should trust the Lord and that it is wonderful to have Christ within us in every circumstance. Isn't that right?"*

Life is a lot of blood, sweat, tears, and dirty little jobs no one else wants to do, Luis realized. *The important thing is not what I do, but who I am. Am I willing to be a faithful servant of Christ, no matter what?*

Three weeks later, Mrs. Palau arrived from Argentina. "Your visit is a godsend, Mom," Luis told her. "Thanks for agreeing to stay with Pat and the kids while I'm in Guatemala."

His trip lasted five weeks. He traveled around Guatemala, preaching in Presbyterian churches, schools, and special meetings. Back home, he told Pat about the wonderful things the Lord had done during that ministry tour. Then he said, "But I've determined that I won't be separated from the whole family for that long a period again, if at all possible."

Summer meant another move for the Palaus. OC field director Ed Murphy needed them in Bogotá, Colombia, to help train the "man in the pew" in how to share his faith, lead others to Christ, disciple new believers, and plant new churches. After a few months in Bogotá, Luis and Ed determined that another city—Cali—would be more receptive to their ministry.

Another move meant adjusting to a different culture. It also meant finding another apartment and another housekeeper (who also doubled as a security guard).

Luis continued to struggle with his temper. One day,

Pat suggested that they take a walk to a nearby park. When a rainstorm later drenched them, Luis blew up. "It was your idea that we take this walk, and now we're soaked."

Pat didn't respond. She knew there was no use trying to argue and reason with an angry man. Weeks later, Luis understood the effects of his temper when he asked Pat where she would like to go during some free time.

"I think you'd better decide where we go this time," Pat replied.

After settling in Cali, the work began. The evangelistic street meetings they planned would be the first these Colombians had seen in ten years. Extreme persecution and violent killings had all but silenced the proclamation of the gospel.

"The local Christians don't want to get involved in evangelism," Luis told Pat, "but I don't blame them. They fear persecution. Preaching in the streets simply isn't done. It's even a bit risky. But change is in the air. I'm convinced that God is going to swing the doors wide open for evangelism in Colombia."

Their first effort was with a Christian and Missionary Alliance church. Bruce Woodman, Luis's old friend from Argentina, who had also worked at HCJB radio in Quito, Ecuador, came and played the trombone and led singing. Afterward, Luis and several others preached the gospel.

One day, Bruce asked Luis, "How would you like to start a daily evangelistic radio program?"

"What?" Luis asked.

"Yes, a daily radio program. All you have to do is travel to Quito every so often to record the programs."

Excited, Luis agreed. Later, he began a daily Bible teaching program, as well. He had no idea that both programs would continue to be broadcast to this day and would help open doors for future crusades and other ministry opportunities all across the Spanish-speaking world.

"Today I'm going to speak about the indwelling Christ as our resource and power to serve," Luis said to the listening group of missionaries. He knew that his team members would chuckle at his chosen topic; he had spoken on it so often. But it had taken him so long to learn the lesson about resting in and relying upon Jesus, that he had to make sure that others knew the secret, too.

Afterward, an old missionary gentleman approached Luis. "I would like to talk with you," he said. "Will you walk with me?"

As they strolled through the conference center grounds, the missionary began to weep. "Luis," he began, "I have been here on the field for more than forty years. I have worked for God as hard as I could, with every ounce of my being, but it has brought me little but frustration. Now I see why."

Wiping his eyes, he continued, "Until today, I don't think I have ever really known what it meant to allow the risen Christ to do the living in me."

The memory of falling to his knees in Multnomah's dormitory swept over Luis. "I know exactly how you feel," Luis said. "Giving it all you've got with little results; feeling bitter and discouraged because you lack victory in your life and ministry. And the release when you finally realize you can rely on the power of the Holy Spirit, rather than on grim determination, to hang on. It sounds too simple, too easy. Yet it's the truth. We have the mind of Christ. With His power, we can rely on Him to give us victory over temptation. We can depend on His strength and wisdom."

As they said their good-byes, the missionary grabbed Luis's hand. "Thank you, brother," he said. "Thank you."

Despite all the God-given successes, Luis felt a twinge of discouragement. *I'm in my thirties now,* he thought. *So many opportunities for mass evangelism are passing me by. I have learned a lot and have such big plans, but I can't do it on my own.*

With those thoughts on his mind, Luis once again approached Dick Hillis, the president of OC, when he visited Colombia.

"Dick, there are great needs for evangelistic work here in the Cali area," Luis said. "Please, let me start my own evangelistic team and begin holding evangelistic crusades."

"We've gone over this ground before," Dick said gently. "You haven't yet completed your first term with OC, and we've started you small so you can learn some things— including humility. We're not ready for you to move ahead with citywide crusades. Besides, you're more of a Bible teacher; Santiago Garabaya is the evangelist on the team."

Luis listened, but disagreed. *Maybe I'm not a great evangelist,* he thought. *Speaking doesn't come easily; I struggle over my messages. But I want to be an evangelist because of the command of Christ. I have long felt the compulsion to preach the gospel. Being a solid Bible teacher shouldn't be a liability and hinder my serving in this area.*

At every turn, Luis continued to press for the opportunity to lead a crusade team within the mission. But the leaders of OC weren't sure he was ready for it yet. And Pat seemed to agree.

In September 1965, Luis was allowed to lead his first local

church campaign at La Floresta Presbyterian Church in Cali. Luis knew that his strategy to reach the cities for Christ began with working in the small, local churches. *With just sixty members, La Floresta qualifies as small,* Luis said to himself.

He decided to spend the first week addressing the spiritual condition of the people in the church. He knew that Christians can't and won't enjoy evangelism and discipleship unless they confess all known sin, experience God's forgiveness, consecrate their lives to the Lord, and begin to enjoy the Christ-centered, Spirit-filled life. Luis's plan was precise and theologically sound, but he nearly didn't get past the second night. Revival broke out!

During the message on confession, a man suddenly stood. "Wait a minute," he said. "This is enough! I'm an elder of this church, but I've got to confess my sins right here. My family is a mess, and I'm a shame to this church. My wife and I don't get along; my children disobey me. Look; I'm seated here, my wife's over there, and my children are back there somewhere."

In tears, the man asked his wife and children to come to him. As they walked to him, people all over the tiny sanctuary began popping to their feet to confess their sins.

Luis watched, speechless and a bit scared. "Lord," he prayed, "I asked for revival, but I wasn't expecting this. I've never experienced anything like this before." For nearly two hours, the Christians in that little church in the middle of nowhere publicly confessed their sins and got right with God.

By the end of two weeks, more than 125 people trusted Christ as their Savior. About eighty joined the congregation. The church was in a state of revival for months to come.

Luis could hardly sleep. He and several others walked around town at night, too excited to sleep, praying, and dreaming big dreams for the future. *If God can do this in one local church, what else can He do?* Luis asked himself.

Two months later, Luis traveled back to Quito and HCJB. That night, he would test a new concept—a live, call-in counseling television broadcast. *Will anyone even call?* Luis wondered, as he settled himself behind the desk in the recording studio. Suddenly, he was on the air. "I'm here to talk with you live, over the phone, about problems or concerns you might have right now," Luis told the viewers.

Luis answered first one call, then another. He never knew what to expect. One person on the verge of suicide would call in. The next person would be going through a messy divorce. Luis always pointed the person to the Bible and to Jesus Christ.

Thank God He has given me the ability to think quickly under pressure and to remember specific Scriptures, Luis thought. *But I need to work even harder at storing up God's answers for all the problems represented by callers from all walks of life.*

Finally, the broadcast ended. Luis was exhausted, but the phones kept ringing. The same thing happened the next night: People kept calling in even after the program went off the air. So Luis and his crew kept the program on the air, longer and longer. After a couple of weeks, they were staying on the air for three hours at a time.

One night, Luis received a call from a young airline stewardess who had seen her parents' marriage break up. She had decided that if her father—a judge on the high court—could live in sin, so could she. And so she did. She was having an affair with a young Colombian doctor. She was miserable, repentant, and desperate to be forgiven.

When Luis read to her from the Bible that God loved her and offered her forgiveness and salvation, she wanted to receive Him right then and there.

He hesitated. *Lord, should I pray with this woman on the air?* he prayed silently. *You know I usually counsel callers from the Scriptures and set up appointments where I can carefully show them the way of salvation at the studio counseling office the next day. But she's desperate and obviously sincere.*

Luis asked her to pray with him and added that anyone else watching by television who wanted to pray along and receive Christ could do so. "Dear God," he began, "I know I am a sinner." She repeated each line. "I have broken a sacred marriage. I have done a hateful thing to a man's wife and children." And they prayed on, recounting the sins she had told Luis. "Father, I need Your forgiveness and Your saving love." It was a tearful, solemn, anointed moment as she prayed to receive Christ.

The young stewardess was so excited that she insisted upon an appointment the next morning at nine.

The next caller was brief. A tiny, high-pitched, squeaky voice simply requested an appointment the next day at nine-thirty. No more conversation. When Luis agreed, the person simply thanked him and hung up.

That meeting turned out to be one of the most bizarre encounters of Luis's ministry.

ten

The next morning, Luis and the young stewardess met to talk about the decision she had made over the phone. Luis encouraged her in her newfound faith and gave her a Bible and some literature.

He walked her to the door and noticed a little woman walking through the gates of the HCJB property, followed closely by two huge, able-bodied men. *Those two guys could be linemen for the Dallas Cowboys,* Luis thought.

As the woman entered the office, Luis asked if the two gentlemen would like to come in, too. "No," the woman said. "One will stand by the door and the other by the gate." Luis recognized the squeaky voice from the night before. A quick look at the clock showed she was right on time.

The woman brushed past Luis and felt along the bottom edges of the desktop, as if looking for something. Without explanation, she moved to the wall and peeked behind a hanging picture. Her eyes traveled to every corner before she finally sat down. *She must be mentally unbalanced,* Luis thought.

When she started talking, Luis knew that this woman was unlike anyone he had ever met. She swore and smoked with a passion. She sucked every last bit from her cigarette, and then lit the next with the smoldering butt of the last.

In spite of her tiny voice, she spoke through a sneer, and venom poured out. Her voice dripped with sarcasm and hatred. "You pastors and priests," she began with disgust. "You are a bunch of thieves and liars and crooks. All you want is to deceive people; all you want is money!"

Her tirade lasted more than twenty minutes. The entire time she swore and accused, criticized and insulted. Her bitterness left Luis speechless. *Lord, how shall I handle this?* he prayed silently.

Seemingly exhausted from her verbal attack, she finally slumped in her chair. She took a deep breath, her eyes still flashing.

"Madam," Luis began, "is there anything I can do for you? How can I help you?"

She slowly took her cigarette from her lips, stared at Luis for an instant, then broke into uncontrollable sobs. *Lord, what am I going to do?* Luis prayed again. *I'm no psychiatrist. I'm just a preacher. Why did You send her to me? She seems insane.*

In a few minutes, when she could speak again, the edge was gone from her voice. "You know," she said, "in the thirty-eight years I have lived, you are the first person who has ever asked if he could help me. All my life, people have come to me with their hands out, saying, 'Help me, come here, do this, go there, do that.' "

"What is your name?" Luis asked.

The woman was suddenly hard again. "Why do you want to know my name?"

"Well, you've said a lot of things here, and I don't even know you. I just want to know how to address you."

She sat back in her chair and straightened up a bit. Cocking her head and looking at Luis out of the corner of her eye, she lifted her chin and took yet another drag of her cigarette. Then she said with finality, "I'm going to tell you," as if gaining such knowledge was a real privilege.

"My name is Maria," she said. Luis recognized her last name as that of a large family of wealth and influence. "I am the secretary of the Communist Party here in Ecuador. I am a Marxist-Leninist, and I am a materialist. I don't believe in God."

With that, she took off on another nonstop tirade against all preachers and priests, the church, the Bible, and anything else she could think of that rivaled her beliefs.

"Why did you come here?" Luis broke in. "Just to insult me, or what?"

She was thoughtful again. "I'm going to tell you my story," she announced.

As a teenager, Maria had rebelled and run away from a religious school. Her parents gave her a choice: Return to school or leave the family. She left. The communists befriended her and took her in. Within the next few years, she married and divorced three times and had several children. Despite her upbringing, she became a party leader and organized student rebellions.

Maria's story played like a grade-B movie. She revealed more and more, interrupting her narrative only occasionally to emphatically remind Luis of her list of titles and beliefs and nonbeliefs. She made it quite clear that, as a

Marxist-Leninist, she opposed everything that Christianity stood for.

Luis let her talk without interruption. He kept praying, *When will she reveal her vulnerability? When will the opening come?* Three hours after she began, the opportunity finally arrived.

"Listen, Palau," Maria said, "supposing there is a God—and I'm not saying there is, because I don't believe in the Bible, and I don't believe there's a God—but just supposing there is. Just for the sake of chatting about it, if there is a God—which there isn't—do you think He would receive a woman like me?"

So this poor, frightened, little woman with the big façade has a chink in her armor, after all! Luis thought. He recalled what he had studied years before in Dr. R. A. Torrey's book *How to Work for Christ:* When dealing with a professed atheist, take one verse from the Bible and stay with it, repeating it as many times as necessary until it sticks.

Which verse suits her? Luis wondered. As he prayed, the Lord reminded him of one of his favorite verses, Hebrews 10:17: " 'Their sins and their lawless deeds I will remember no more' " (NKJV).

He said, "Look, Maria, don't worry about what I think; look at what God thinks." He opened to the verse and turned the Bible so she could see it.

"But I don't believe in the Bi—"

"You've already told me that," he said. "But we're just supposing there's a God, right? Let's just suppose this is His Word. He says, 'Their sins and their lawless deeds I will remember no more.' "

She waited, as if there had to be more. Luis said nothing. "But, listen; I've been an adulteress, married three times, and in bed with a lot of different men."

Luis repeated, " 'Their sins and their lawless deeds I will remember no more.' "

"But I haven't told you half my story. I stabbed a comrade who later committed suicide."

" 'Their sins and their lawless deeds I will remember no more.' "

"I've led student riots where people were killed!"

" 'Their sins and their lawless deeds I will remember no more.' "

"I egged on my friends and then hid while they were out dying for the cause."

" 'Their sins and their lawless deeds I will remember no more.' "

Seventeen times Luis responded to Maria's objections and confessions with that one Bible verse. It was past lunchtime. Tired and weak, Luis finally said, "Would you like Christ to forgive all that you've told me about, and all the rest that I don't even know?"

Maria was quiet. Finally she spoke softly, "If He could forgive me and change me, it would be the greatest miracle in the world." Luis led her in a simple prayer of commitment. By the end, she was crying.

A week later, Maria returned to tell Luis that she was reading the Bible and that she felt a lot better. A longtime missionary from HCJB agreed to follow up with her since Luis was returning to Colombia.

Two months passed. In January 1966, Luis decided he should return to Quito for more television counseling and radio-program taping before the birth of their third son, Andrew, who was due in a month. While there, he was again visited by Maria. Her face was purple and bruised and several front teeth were missing.

"Maria, what happened?" Luis asked.

"Shortly after our last visit, I went to a meeting of all the communist leaders of the country," Maria said. "I told them, 'I am no longer an atheist. I believe in God and in Jesus Christ, and I have become a Christian. I am resigning from the party, and I don't want to have anything more to do with it. We are all a bunch of liars. We deceive people when we tell them there is no God. Of course there is a God! Look at the garden outside. Do you think the flowers created themselves? Are you going to tell me everything is the result of some explosion in space billions of years ago?' "

"How did they react to your announcement?" Luis asked.

"It was as if I had let a bunch of hungry lions out of a cage," Maria replied. "The leaders fought among themselves, some trying to shout me down and get at me, another insisting that I should be allowed to speak. A few days later, I was nearly run down by a Jeep full of my former comrades. The next day, several of my former protégés—militant university students—attacked me and smashed my face against a utility pole until I was unconscious."

Maria continued, "I was forced to hide out in the basements of several churches and in the homes of missionaries, always on the run. For me and the HCJB missionary to be able to study the Bible, we first had to drive around until we were sure no one was following us."

Luis listened in silence, amazed at the persecution she had suffered as such a young believer.

"There's going to be a revolution in June," she told him matter-of-factly. "The Party has had it all planned for months."

She explained that students and agitators would cause a disturbance in the streets, luring out the army, which would then be attacked and, if possible, overthrown. The military junta then would be forced to leave the country, and the chairman of the Communist Party for Ecuador would come out of hiding in Colombia and take over the country.

When Maria left, she again went into hiding, remaining on the run until June. On the morning of the revolution, the Communist Party leader came out of Colombia to talk to her. In a few hours he was to become the new ruler of the country, but first he wanted to talk to his longtime friend.

"Maria," he asked, "why did you become a Christian?"

"Because I believe in God and in Jesus Christ, and my faith has changed my life."

"You know," he said, "while hiding out, I have been listening to HCJB radio on shortwave, and those—they almost have me believing there is a God!"

"There is!" she said. "Why don't you become a Christian and get out of this business? We never had any real convictions about atheism and materialism. And look at all the lives we've ruined and all the terrible things we've been into. Here, take this Bible and this book [*Peace with God,* by Billy Graham]. You can go to my father's farm and read them."

Miraculously, he accepted her offer. Later that morning, the disturbance that was supposed to trigger a revolution fizzled into chaos, and Ecuador was saved from anarchy, tyranny, and worse.

Maria's story may be wild, but her conversion had an effect on the history of an entire country. Seeing what God did with Maria solidified Luis's burden, not just for individuals, but also for nations.

eleven

We have to clip Luis's wings!" one of the OC board members said when he returned from a trip to Colombia. As usual, Luis had waylaid this member to talk to him about "turning the corner and getting into some true citywide evangelism."

It was all field director Ed Murphy and the whole OC staff could do to put up with the constant reminders from Luis: "Life is going by too fast. I want to redeem the time. I'm more than thirty years old!"

Luis shared his frustrations with Ray Stedman, who had flown in for a visit after attending a pastors' conference in Guatemala. "I'm getting desperate to get moving," Luis said. "I know it's going to take several years to expand beyond local church campaigns to united citywide evangelistic crusades. If I let the years slip by, I'll be an old man, still hoping and dreaming foolish dreams. I don't want that to happen."

"Be patient," Ray said simply.

"Be patient?" Luis said in frustration. "How long must I sit around and sit around? If I have to leave OC and start on my own from scratch, I may do it."

"Be patient," Ray repeated. "If God is in it, it will happen when the time is right."

Late in 1966, Luis began receiving letters from OC board member Vic Whetzel about considering Mexico as a fertile ground for mass evangelism. When mentioning the correspondence to Pat, Luis said, "I wonder what he's driving at? Maybe we will be asked to switch mission fields."

Those thoughts kept Luis company during a flight to Berlin, Germany, for the World Congress on Evangelism. One dark, cold afternoon, when the congress meetings had let out early and many of the 1,200 delegates were milling around West Berlin, Luis received a call from OC board members Dr. Ray Benson and Dr. Dick Hillis. "Let's take a walk, Luis. We need to chat."

Bundled in his overcoat, Luis trudged alongside the two men. *Come on, fellows,* Luis thought. *It's cold out here. We've been walking for what seems like miles. Get to the point.*

Finally, Dr. Hillis said, "Luis, we feel that you and Pat should go home on furlough in December as planned. Once your furlough is over, begin to develop your own evangelistic team with your sights set on Mexico. You'll be field director for Mexico, with your headquarters there."

Luis was speechless. *My dream has come true!* Then he started asking questions. "Will I be able to have Joe Lathrop on my team? We're going to need a music man; can we arrange for Bruce Woodman to work with us?"

Dr. Hillis and Dr. Benson agreed readily. Then Dr. Hillis told Luis, "I hope you will become the greatest evangelist in the world."

Luis knew immediately what he meant—Dr. Hillis wanted nothing for Luis's glory, everything for God's glory. *So do I,* Luis said to himself. *So do I.*

Just before leaving Colombia on furlough, the Palaus stopped in Bogotá for their first citywide crusade. Luis had promised a national organization of Christian young people that he would be there for a parade and a four-day crusade, December 8 to 12, 1966. "Even if we get killed, come what may, we'll do it," they told him, "if you'll help us." They knew the rally could shake up their country and bring to it an awareness of the gospel.

The youth leaders had done their work well. Thousands of Christians from surrounding towns converged on the capital city on December 8 for a parade. They lined up with no more than four people in a row, stretching out for twelve city blocks. Everyone carried a Bible and a small transistor radio.

The Bible they held over their hearts, expressing how highly they esteemed the Word of God. By their actions they were also saying: "I dare you to come and kill me."

The radios were tuned to one of the local stations that was broadcasting a selection of Christian songs. This way the singing would be synchronized all the way down the line as seven thousand young people marched from the Intercontinental Hotel down Seventh Avenue to Bolivar Plaza, a huge square bordered by government offices and the main cathedral.

What an impressive sight, Luis said to himself as the parade got under way. But it was also a little scary and more than a little dangerous. Anything could happen. Suddenly, Luis saw red lights flashing. Police cars were coming. Many of the marchers froze.

So this is it, Luis thought as he motioned for Pat to get herself and the boys out of harm's way. *God, make it quick.* But to the surprise of everyone, the police cars maneuvered to the front of the parade, red lights still flashing, and led the marchers down the avenue, helping clear the way.

Luis felt the mood lighten as the thousands of young people realized that the parade was a great success. The singing grew louder, the smiles broader, the steps lighter. Posters and banners with Bible verses swung in the air with more enthusiasm than ever.

Luis silently cheered as many older Christians joined in the march—including a group of missionaries and national pastors who had been looking on from a safe distance. Half a dozen priests and a group of nuns also fell in step.

The crowds continued to grow. Twelve thousand people followed the parade to Bolivar Plaza, creating such a stir that the archbishop peeked out his cathedral window.

The president even came out of his office. He asked what was going on, then said to one of the youth leaders, "If you can draw a crowd like this, you could get a president elected."

Standing on the stairway of the main government building, Luis began to speak to the twenty thousand people who had jammed the plaza. At the end of his brief message, three hundred people raised their hands, publicly committing their lives to Jesus Christ, and several hundred more were saved during the crusade meetings over the next four nights.

"God, this has been a historic moment for Colombia

and for all of Latin America," Luis prayed. "Never before have people committed to Christ made such a dramatic impact in this country. A new era has begun. Thank You.

"This has also been a historic moment for me. I no longer have to fret, waiting for my chance to get into crusade evangelism on a larger scale. By Your grace, we are on our way. I can't think of a better way to end one missionary term and start looking forward to the next!"

twelve

Furlough meant two things to Luis and Pat: time with family and deputation work. For a year and a half, they visited churches and spoke at conferences, doing all they could to spread the word everywhere that Luis had a new team and was ready to share Christ's message in Mexico.

Luis was excited to again visit Peninsula Bible Church in Palo Alto. He was scheduled to speak at their annual missions conference, but his lunch appointment with several men from Stanford University left a strong impression on him.

As he talked about the results he'd seen in Colombia and his dreams for Mexico, one professor looked him in the eye and asked, point-blank: "Palau, how can you go to country after country, where people have such vast economic and social problems, and preach about the resurrected Christ? Can't you do something more practical for them?"

"There isn't a better way to help them," Luis replied. "The people of this world create the problems of this world. If we can lead them to Christ, we will create a climate for other positive, practical changes to take place."

Over and over again I'm asked that question, Luis thought later. *I wish I could make them understand. I'm not against social activism. It's a good thing to do. But if we want to see people turned around, they've got to have Christ in their hearts. He is the only One who can change lives.*

Eager to share Christ with the people of Mexico, Luis could hardly wait for their furlough to end. In mid-1968, the Palaus finally arrived at their new field of ministry and began to settle in to their apartment. It didn't take long, because their furniture had not yet arrived. But the inconvenience didn't dampen their high hopes.

After a local church campaign in Mexico City, Luis flew to Colombia for back-to-back crusades in three of the largest cities. During the last one, in Medellín, the local crusade committee approached Luis and said, "This is going so well; let's have another week of meetings."

A brief battle raged within him. *But I want to go back to Mexico City,* Luis argued silently with himself. *I wish I had the guts to tell them that. I miss Pat and the boys. Then there are those free tickets. I doubt I'll ever again be living in a city that is hosting the Summer Olympics with tickets to attend my favorite events.*

Luis quickly set aside his selfish thoughts. *Palau, you may be missing a once-in-a-lifetime opportunity, but it's because you will be helping others make a once-in-a-lifetime decision.* As he agreed to stay, he couldn't help but think of what the apostle Paul wrote:

"Do you not know that in a race all the runners run, but only one gets the prize? Run in such a way as to get the prize. Everyone who competes in the [Olympic] games goes into strict training. They do it to get a crown that will not last; but we do it to get a crown that will last forever (1 Corinthians 9:24–25).

Still, Luis felt loneliness and regret that he wasn't home with his family. As he looked through his Bible one night, a verse jumped out at him. He read, "All your sons shall be taught by the LORD, and great shall be the prosperity of your sons" (Isaiah 54:13 RSV).

"I believe that the Lord gave me that verse tonight," Luis said. "Those words are a promise from God. I'm going to claim that verse for my sons."

A week later, when Luis arrived home, the apartment looked as bare as the day they had moved in. He soon discovered that a colossal transportation snafu meant they had to go without furniture for months on end. A tough adjustment was made even tougher for Pat, who had to learn another culture and another distinct way of speaking Spanish. On top of that, she had her hands full with three growing boys and another soon on the way.

This is more than any woman should have to bear, Luis thought. So he picked up the phone and called Pat's mom. The plan was for her to call and invite Pat and the kids to Portland for four to six weeks. "I'll pay for everything," Luis said. "Just don't let Pat know that it was my idea."

Throughout 1969, Luis and team members Joe Lathrop and John McWilliam kept a rapid pace. They staged fourteen campaigns in Mexico alone. The largest one was in a bullring in Monterrey, where more than thirty thousand heard the gospel in nine days, and two thousand made decisions for Christ—including José, the printer who produced the crusade advertising.

Luis was especially impressed by a young pastor whose church was in a rough "drugs-and-muggings" neighborhood in Monterrey. Fresh out of Bible college, he totally immersed his tiny congregation in the crusade. They invited drug addicts, prostitutes, everyone they could to the meetings. By the end of the crusade, fifteen new families were added to the church. One drug addict who was converted through the witness of that congregation later became pastor of a church in a nearby city.

Exciting crusades and the blessing of many conversions left Luis ecstatic. But those days were also some of the roughest in his ministry. He often found himself waiting and hoping and praying for money to come in, wondering why his family had to live at such an impractical level.

Then discouragement hit. A gigantic crusade the team had planned for and promoted at a baseball park in Mexico City was canceled at the last minute by the government. *Will we ever get on our feet?* Luis wondered. *Yes, we will. God wants us here and we are going to have that big crusade in Mexico City, somehow, someway, even with the baseball park off-limits.*

The team came up with a plan. They scheduled crusade meetings in two of the oldest and most respected Protestant churches in Mexico City, which happened to stand back-to-back. Each night, Luis would finish his evangelistic message in one church, rush out the back door, and hurry into the second church in time to start preaching again.

After the fifteenth and final night, Luis collapsed, exhausted, on his bed. But the crazy plan worked. God allowed him to see more than two thousand people make public commitments to Christ.

In the years that followed, Luis was able to meet some of the decision-makers from those impromptu, simultaneous crusades in the heart of Mexico City. One woman had been a night club singer in Mexico City. After trusting Jesus Christ, she joined a local church and grew in her faith. Five years later, she served as a soloist at the Luis Palau Netzahualcóyotl crusade just east of Mexico City.

Another decision-maker had been a gung-ho Marxist-Leninist university student. He became attracted to a quiet, sweet fellow university student and began spending all his free time with her.

One day she said, "Carlos, come with me to a youth meeting."

"What's it about?"

"Youth and sex."

"Let's go!"

Carlos didn't know he was attending a crusade until the singing began. *Religious stuff!* he thought, and almost stomped out. But the subject of sex intrigued him, so he stayed. As Luis preached, the words from the Bible gripped his mind, and he made a decision to follow Jesus Christ. The change in his life was instantaneous. He immediately rejected communism, joined a local church, was baptized, took the discipleship training offered by Campus Crusade for Christ, and led more than 120 other people to Christ while working on his psychology degree.

Although Luis had yet to hear these stories, he knew that the spiritual fruit harvested from the Mexico City crusade would last.

That November, Pat and Luis went to the hospital for the birth of their fourth son, Stephen, then geared up for another full year of evangelism in 1970.

The first crusade of the new year was in El Salvador's capital. Luis kept an exhausting pace each day, racing from one speaking engagement to another. Even nighttime brought little opportunity to rest as he hurried from the stadium after the meetings and arrived at the studios of Channel 4 for his live television counseling program.

One evening, Bruce Woodman and Luis arrived at the hotel, hoping for a good night's sleep. Luis had just entered his room when the phone rang. Picking it up, Luis heard the desk clerk's voice: "Sorry to disturb you, sir, but someone in the lobby is anxious to talk with you."

Luis looked at the clock. *It's 1:45 A.M.,* he thought in irritation. *I've been up since 7:00 yesterday morning, and now some guy, most likely a drunk, wants to talk!*

Luis called Bruce, and they went down to the lobby together. A distinguished-looking gentleman hurried up to them. He was visibly shaking. "I watched your program three hours ago," he said, "and it hit home to my problem. I began to weep and my teenage daughter said, 'Dad, why don't you go and talk to him? He might be able to help you with your drinking problem.' "

Luis and Bruce listened as the man also confessed to being persistently unfaithful to his wife. He then revealed that he was a well-known psychologist who counseled others. "I can't control myself. I'm living like a dog!" He pounded his fist on the coffee table, then pleaded: "Is there any hope of change for a hypocrite like me?"

Several people in the hotel bar had heard the disturbance and now stood in the lobby watching from a distance. Bruce and Luis told the less-than-sober psychologist about Jesus Christ and His almighty power. Finally the man said, "I want to receive Christ right now." Ignoring the onlookers, he fell to his knees in the middle of the lobby, and the two evangelists led him in prayer.

A week later, during the final live television broadcast, Luis answered the last phone call of the night.

"Mr. Palau," the voice said, "do you remember the man you talked to at 3:00 in the morning in the hotel? That's me."

Luis asked, "Have you experienced any change this past week?"

"A complete change! And now my wife is here to talk to you."

I can't believe this is happening, Luis thought. *This conversation is being broadcast across the entire nation of El Salvador.* When the wife got on the phone, he asked, "Have you seen a change in your husband this past week?"

Not only had she, but now she wanted to receive Christ! Her prayer of conversion was heard by an estimated audience of 450,000.

Back in Mexico, Luis and the team could only dream of getting on television. Even holding large-scale crusades seemed next to impossible. When they heard that another religious group had drawn a large crowd to a convention, they decided to call their next Mexico City crusade a convention, too. Another strategy they used was to advertise only over radio programs and by word-of-mouth so that the authorities wouldn't shut them down again.

When Luis heard the final statistics of the ten-day crusade, he was overwhelmed. More than 106,000 people attended the convention, and nearly 6,675 people committed their lives to Christ. Churches doubled in size almost overnight. Never before had he seen such a great response to the gospel.

It's finally happening, after all these years, Luis thought to himself. *Ever since I was a teen, I've dreamed of helping change the world. Slowly but surely, my dream is becoming a reality. Years of hard work and perseverance are starting to pay off. We're reaching the masses!*

The word began to spread that God was doing great things south of the border. One journalist reporting on the crusade's impact called Luis "the Billy Graham of Latin America." The moniker stuck.

Luis knew that if he was going to keep up the same excruciating crusade schedule, he needed all the help he could get. But when OC sent Jim Williams—a graduate of Biola College and Talbot Theological Seminary—to join his team later in 1970, Luis was upset. He fired off a letter, asking why he hadn't been given a chance to interview Jim, let alone get to know him. Then, when Jim arrived, he seemed so quiet and hadn't yet learned Spanish fluently. So off went another letter of complaint.

It wasn't long before Luis came to value Jim as a member of the team. Jim soon mastered Spanish and became an expert in biblical counseling. He also proved to be an excellent theologian. Luis had no idea of the future role that Jim would play at the Luis Palau Evangelistic Association. (He now serves as vice president of Latin American ministries for LPEA.)

With more men under his leadership, Luis began to understand the "patience" speech he'd heard repeatedly several years earlier. That's why he made an unusual request during one visit to OC headquarters in California. Luis called ahead and asked if Ed Murphy would meet him at the airport.

In the car, he told Ed, "I asked for you to meet me because I want to apologize, Ed, for treating you unfairly when I was a missionary in Colombia."

Ed almost fainted at Luis's words, and he tried to apologize for some of the difficulties.

Luis stopped him. "No, I'm a director now, and I have a team full of young, headstrong men. I don't know how you ever put up with me. I was selfish and critical of you. Will you forgive me?" Luis also apologized publicly at OC headquarters during their international strategy meetings.

Back home in Mexico, Luis faced other, more difficult apologies. He sensed that something was amiss between him and one of the twins, Keith. So Luis called Keith into his office and asked, "Keith, have I done anything that really hurt your feelings?"

Instantly, Keith said, "Yes. Last Christmas you promised to buy me a toy submachine gun and you never gave it to me."

Luis had forgotten all about the toy. He probed further: "Is there anything else I've done that wasn't right and I've never asked for your forgiveness?"

Again, instantly, Keith said, "Yes."

"And what was that?"

"Remember when Mom said you had to go to the hospital because Stephen was going to be born? You left us at home and took off in a hurry. Remember?"

Luis nodded.

"Well, you took off, you left Mom at the hospital, and you forgot the suitcase with all the stuff. So you came back and you were real huffy. When you got here, the suitcase had been opened and everything was thrown all over the place. And you spanked me."

Luis felt his heart sink. "And you didn't do it?" he asked Keith.

"No, I didn't."

Luis felt terrible. He pulled Keith near, gave him a hug, and asked his forgiveness. That same day, Luis saw an improvement in their relationship.

That went so well that I think I'll call in Kevin, Luis said to himself. *After all, maybe I've hurt him, too.*

When Kevin sat down, Luis asked, "Have I ever done something wrong and never asked your forgiveness or promised you something and never fulfilled my promise?"

Without any hesitation, Kevin said, "Yes."

"What was it?"

"Last Christmas you promised us a toy submachine gun and you never bought it for us." Kevin had no idea that a few minutes earlier Luis had talked to Keith about the same thing. That day, Luis took his sons to the store and bought them what he had promised.

Many times before leaving on a ministry trip, Luis would think, *It just isn't worth leaving my family, unless some souls are saved.* To be gone so much of the time from Pat and the boys was never easy. Even harder was coming back home knowing that he had to turn around and leave again in a few days. Sometimes trying to fulfill all his obligations as a husband and father and an evangelist seemed impossible. The only way he could justify the time apart was knowing that people were coming to the Lord.

One especially agonizing separation came late in 1970. Luis was leaving for Peru, a nation on the brink of a leftist takeover. Guerrilla warfare and bloodshed were common. In the midst of the chaos, Luis and his team had been invited to hold a large evangelistic crusade in the capital city. Preparations were in full swing, and Luis felt compelled to preach at some pre-crusade rallies before the situation worsened. He wouldn't find out until years later how his trip changed the life of one Rosario Rivera.

thirteen

Rosario was born out of wedlock in the slums outside Lima, Peru. She grew up filled with anger at the lack of food and water and the poverty all around her.

Although she never finished school, Rosario read as much and as often as she could. By age thirteen, she was reading Marx and Lenin. By the time she was eighteen, she had become a militant communist.

While training in Cuba, Rosario met the famous revolutionary Che Guevara and became his assistant. He filled her with a passion for her country and humanity.

Before Guevara went on a mission to Bolivia, he asked Rosario to survey the situation for him. She warned him not to go to Bolivia, but he ignored her advice and met a violent death.

Death was nothing new to Rosario. She hated the upper classes and anyone else who stood in her way; she despised anything to do with God or Christianity. She killed without remorse during her missions.

In December 1970, Rosario returned to Lima. This bitter, angry, callous woman had a mission to accomplish. As she listened to the radio one day, she heard Luis and found out he would be speaking live at a theater that evening. She was furious. She didn't know Luis, but that didn't matter. Because he talked about God, she hated him.

She entered the theater where Luis was speaking about the "Five Hells of Human Existence"—murder, robbery, deceit, hypocritical homes, and hatred. Each sin Luis mentioned pricked Rosario's conscience. At the invitation, Rosario came forward with scores of other people. She wasn't thinking of conversion—murder was on her mind.

A counselor, a little old Peruvian lady, saw Rosario and approached her. She asked, "Madam, can I help you receive Christ?"

Rosario slapped the poor woman, then panicked at the commotion she caused and ran from the theater.

Rosario couldn't sleep that night. She tossed and turned, her mind whirling with images from the crusade. She kept hearing Luis quote two Bible verses: "Cursed is the one who trusts in man, who depends on flesh for his strength and whose heart turns away from the LORD," and "Blessed is the man who trusts in the LORD, whose confidence is in him" (Jeremiah 17:5, 7).

Very early the next morning, Rosario fell to her knees as a hardened criminal, and stood back up as a child of God.

Her communist comrades came looking for her. She machine-gunned them with Scriptures, and when they left, she thanked God that His Spirit would work in them.

Thirty years later, Rosario is still a revolutionary. She

continues to work for social change in Peru, but now by the power of the Spirit of God. "If my heart burned for the revolution in the past, then it burns even more now, and if I did a lot for the poor before, then I do more now," she said. The poor neighborhood where she came from, for instance, now has running water and electric lights, thanks to her efforts.

Rosario addresses high school classes, meets with factory bosses, and debates political matters, showing that only Christ can meet man's deepest needs. Many young people have received Christ as a result of her ministry. Her social concern and Christian love have challenged churches throughout Peru to move into society with God's Word.

Luis read about Rosario's conversion in a German news service dispatch ten years after the pre-crusade rallies in Lima. When he finally met her during another crusade in Lima a few years later, he said to himself, *Political revolutions never change lives for the better. The only revolution that works occurs every time someone becomes a new creation in Christ. He alone changes lives for good here and now—and for all eternity.*

fourteen

L ord, I'm not sure what to expect," Luis prayed during his return to Lima a few months into 1971. "Politically, things haven't improved. But You are in control of everything, and You can open wide the doors for evangelism."

Two weeks later, Luis praised God for doing more than he had asked or even imagined. The city's large bullring accommodated more than 103,000 people during the crusade. Nearly five thousand people made public commitments to Jesus Christ. And a press conference—unheard of for anything evangelistic—drew forty-two newsmen to a city center hotel.

"Can you believe it?" Luis exclaimed to Pat later. "Forty-two reporters. In the past, Christians have been ridiculed by the media—or simply ignored. But we received nationwide news coverage, and excerpts from my messages aired on fifty-five radio stations. We've finally harnessed the secular media to spread the good news of salvation in Jesus Christ. To God be the glory!"

Luis soon discovered that all the media coverage had created a bridge of sorts to reach out to those in the highest levels of society. In Guatemala that same year, the president, Colonel Carlos Arana Osorio asked Luis for a personal interview. For twenty-five minutes, they met to talk about how Christianity builds a nation. "It's simply through changed individuals," Luis told the president. "Changed individuals who in turn, in their own place and according to their social and educational positions, live a just, hard-working, and 'love-your-neighbor' life."

Luis also met with the mayor of Guatemala City, the U.S. ambassador to Guatemala, and top military officers. In twenty-two days, he preached to nearly 130,000 people, with more than 3,100 trusting Christ as Savior.

Reporters hounded Luis, clamoring for interviews. The nation's leading newspaper reported on the crusade almost every day, even quoting Scripture. One radio interview Luis did was broadcast more than sixty times on eight separate national stations in a single day.

The national impact of the crusade created such excitement in an English-speaking church in the city that they raised enough money to pay for ten weekly programs to be broadcast on secular television immediately following the crusade.

"This is God's hour of visitation, and we dare not let the new opportunities pass us by," Luis wrote to prayer partners and supporters back home.

"We are expecting great things from God. Let's praise Him together for what He will surely do. These are great days to be alive. Dangerous, but exciting. Fruitful, in spite of the confusion and problems. Days of harvest. A fleeting hour of opportunity for us to 'buy up' and to redeem. Praise God for what He is doing and is yet about to do!"

He added, "We are facing the whitest harvest field we have ever known. We must put in the sickle now. But you and I cannot do it alone."

Putting his pen down, Luis thought, *No, we can't do it alone. Not if we are going to create a God-consciousness in every city, every nation where we minister. But by harnessing the power of the media, virtually everyone can hear the gospel. The proof of that can be seen in both Lima and Guatemala City.*

The next year, 1972, Luis faced the greatest test of his entire ministry to that point. He had been invited for a crusade in San Jose, the capital of Costa Rica, but many local Christians didn't want to get involved. The team battled indifference and opposition every step of the way. Still, God poured out His best recompense: tens of thousands filled the bullring and more than 3,200 boys and girls, youths, and adults were converted to Jesus Christ.

One of those converts was Raul Vargas. This miserable young man endured his parents' fighting, jealousy, and adultery. He cried himself to sleep at night, almost overwhelmed by the deep loneliness in his soul.

One day Raul met some Christians, who gave him a Spanish New Testament, which he started to read. Then, after work one evening, Raul saw a poster: "Today, Luis Palau. Free admission." He had no money for the bus, so he walked the mile to the Plaza de Toros. The Holy Spirit spoke to his heart that night, but he left without making a decision. The next night, he returned to the bullring and listened as Luis preached from 2 Corinthians 5:17, which says, "If anyone is in Christ, he is a new creation; the old has gone, the new has come!" By the end of the message, Raul had made a decision to trust Jesus Christ.

Nineteen years passed before Luis met Raul, who smothered him with a big Latin hug. "I'm now a pastor," he told Luis. "I serve at Oasis de Esperanza, the largest evangelical church in Costa Rica, and have helped show hundreds of people the way to Jesus. Thank you. For there, at the Plaza de Toros, the worldly Raul died—not overcome by a bull, but by God's Word!"

Another battle occurred a few months later in western Guatemala. This time the team waged war with the Christian leaders. Galo Vasquez, the crusade director for the team, told Luis that he confronted two pastors whose brawls with each other threatened to derail the crusades. The result? The Presbyterian pastor's son was married—to everyone's astonishment—at the Baptist church. The pastors performed the ceremony together, publicly clearing the air.

Equally as serious, the crusade committee in Coatepeque told Luis, "The mayor is an open atheist. He'll never turn out for the crusade meetings, and it's no use even attempting an interview. He wouldn't accept."

Lord, I know you are as grieved by their grim faithlessness as I am, Luis prayed silently. *Please show them what You can do.*

On the crusade's opening night, Luis watched as more than one-third of the city gathered in the stadium, including the supposedly atheist mayor.

"Would you like to step up and sit on the platform with the evangelist?" one of Luis's team members asked.

"Why, yes!" he said grinning. "I certainly would."

"You know," he leaned over and told Luis as they sat on the platform together, "in all this city's history, never has a crowd like this ever gathered—not even when our president came out west."

"Would you like to address the crowd tonight?" Luis asked.

The mayor agreed and proceeded to give a warm, stirring welcome.

I hope you crusade guys are listening, Luis said to himself.

When he sat down again, the mayor asked Luis to come to city hall to visit him the next day. He wanted to know more about the Bible, was concerned about the future of his three children, and was as friendly as could be.

"Latin Americans are coming alive to the gospel just as I dreamed, Lord," Luis prayed one day. "I used to wonder when my opportunity to do crusade evangelism would come. Now I lament my inability to accept all the crusade invitations coming my way. There's a continent to win. Even with a team, I can do only so much. God, help me come up with some strategies to reach the millions."

The results of that prayer were twofold. Luis began to cultivate associate evangelists within the team—choice, gifted servants of God, who could help spread the gospel. Many of these men now have their own ministries and teams.

The Palau team also started producing evangelistic films that could be used by the local church as an outreach tool or by missionaries starting a new work. "We can't bring 250 million Spanish people to a bullring to hear the gospel," Luis told his team, "but we can take the same transforming message from a bullring to millions of people all across the continent."

Early in 1973, the team broadcast its first live English-language television programs in conjunction with a back-to-back crusade along the Texas-Mexico border. The two-pronged strategy worked well, reaching many diverse people groups throughout the greater McAllen-Reynosa area. Some were rich, some dirt poor; some on the Texas side spoke only Spanish, some on the Mexican side, especially the young people, were fluent in both Spanish and English. When the campaign of contrasts ended, more than eleven hundred Mexicans and Americans had trusted Christ as Savior.

A few weeks later, guerrillas attempted to overthrow the government of the Dominican Republic. "It's only one-and-a-half months before our scheduled campaign in Santo Domingo, the capital there," Luis said to crusade director John McWilliam. "In your opinion, should we go forward with the meetings?"

"Yes, I believe we should," John replied. "The local crusade committee believes that God will see things through."

Often as not during the next few weeks, Luis and the team could be found on their knees praying for wisdom and safety and protection.

Luis arrived in Santo Domingo as planned, excited about the twelve-day crusade. After a special evangelistic breakfast for political leaders and key members of the community, Luis was approached by a lawyer. She had been sent as the president's representative and had a message for Luis.

"The president would like to meet with you before you leave the country," she told him. "But he can only see you on Sunday, immediately after mass, in the chapel of the presidential palace. If you come to mass with him, he will have forty-five minutes to talk with you. His chauffeur will pick you up at 8:30 Sunday morning."

"I'll be there!" Luis said. He was going to speak to the president. *To my knowledge, no one has ever witnessed to this man before,* Luis thought. *What an exciting opportunity for the gospel in the Dominican Republic!*

Before long, however, Luis began to have second thoughts. "Some non-Catholic Christians might hear about me sitting through mass and become upset with me. I can't go through with this."

Luis told a couple of trusted pastors what had happened. "No, Luis," they counseled him, "you must not go. You can't chance it, not with the crusade and all."

In his heart, Luis knew what the Lord wanted him to do. He knew he should go to mass and witness to the president. But he was afraid. On Sunday morning, he watched the limousine drive up outside the hotel. When the chauffeur called for him, fear won the battle. Luis sent him away.

Discouragement swept over Luis. That afternoon, he dropped to his knees and prayed, "Lord, forgive me; I'll never turn down an opportunity to witness to somebody because I fear what others might think."

His personal failure aside, Luis considered the Santo Domingo crusade a success for the Lord. Some seventy thousand people attended the evening meetings. And nearly twenty-four hundred people publicly committed their lives to Christ.

A smaller crusade that same year in the Mexican town of Obregón held great rewards for Luis and the team. "I have rarely seen a place so hungry for the Word of God," Luis later said. "Everywhere we moved about the city— in shops, stores, restaurants, even on the street—we were leading needy people to Christ right and left.

"One bookshop owner sensed the God-consciousness sweeping the area and offered to place evangelistic books in his 102 bookshops all over the three northwestern Mexican states, opening up yet another avenue of sharing the gospel with the masses."

In anticipation of upcoming crusades, Luis also spoke at pastors' conferences and evangelistic rallies in Bolivia and Ecuador. In trepidation, he boarded a very old one-engine Cessna airplane for the last leg of the first trip. The single-engine airplane tossed him up and down and side to side with every bit of turbulence. At times, he caught himself sucking his breath to help them skim just over the top of the massive, razor-sharp Andes mountain ridges. His prayers intensified when he heard the weathered Australian missionary pilot mutter: "Do you think I like flying such a dangerous route in such a small plane? If my boss hadn't sent me, I never would have attempted it."

"I could have choked the missionary who shoved me into that floating piece of cardboard and single propeller," Luis said later, "but it definitely was worth those ninety minutes of terror."

He remembered what one Bolivian pastor had told him as they walked toward the dining room. "I arrived at this conference flat on my face. Two weeks ago, Brother Luis, I was ready to quit the pastorate. I'd had it. Too much criticism, too many discouragements, too much sin in my life. . ."

"And now, Don Carlos?" Luis probed. "Are you quitting?"

"Not on your life! Now I know what victory is all about. Now I see what I can do to equip the people in my church for ministry. Now I have the vision of a crusade to prepare for!"

After his most recent airborne experience, Luis boarded the jumbo jet with thanks to God. He was on his way to

Ecuador, sixteen hundred miles away, for yet another pastors' conference, and then back to Mexico City to celebrate Christmas with Pat and the boys. *I love those big wings!* he thought as he looked out the window during the flight.

As 1973 drew to a close, Luis realized with a start that he and Pat had been on the mission field for ten years. So much had happened since the end of their first term in Colombia, let alone since that first difficult Christmas in Costa Rica back in 1963.

The most exciting days, however, were still ahead.

fifteen

Chaos struck Bolivia in the spring of 1974—the very week that Luis and his team were supposed to have that nation's first Presidential Prayer Breakfast. "The gospel is relevant, no matter what the situation," Luis said, and he boarded the plane for La Paz despite the recent one hundred percent food price increases, riots, a presidential cabinet crisis that saw three ministers resign, a massive rainstorm and flooding, and a "disaster area" proclamation.

After the breakfast, Luis stood in front of the 125 dignitaries, including the Bolivian president, General Hugo Banzer, the Bolivian secretary of state, the chief justice of the Supreme Court, the air force chief of staff, and the mayor of La Paz.

Taking up the theme of crisis, Luis challenged the leaders, "Never give up the battle for righteous government. Take a look at the Bible. It tells us that it's impossible to govern a nation without God (2 Chronicles 7:14), that prayer is talking to God (John 16:24), and that to be heard by God, 'we must be on God's side,' as Abraham Lincoln used to say. That means we must be born again (John3:3–5)." Then Luis concluded the breakfast with a prayer for Bolivia.

Afterward, Bolivia's grateful president asked Luis, "What can I do to help you reach my nation with the gospel?"

"This fall, we'll be returning to Bolivia for three back-to-back evangelistic crusades," Luis replied. "It would be great to have your support. Right now, however, I would love to share the gospel on television through our live, call-in counseling program."

"How long do you need?"

"Ten nights would be good."

"You've got it," the president said as he called his aide over to arrange the national television broadcast. "Ten nights, starting tonight, and all for free."

That evening, Luis and Chester Schemper, South American director of the Bible League, left for the television studios. As they chatted in the taxi, Luis said, "What we really need is three thousand of your New Testaments to give away to the TV viewers."

"And who's going to pay for them?"

"All your rich American supporters!" Luis joked.

The first caller that Luis counseled was a thirty-year-old father of three whose wife had left him. "I'm desperate," he told Luis. "I need some answers." In a short while, he prayed and gave his heart to Christ.

"Do you have a Bible?" Luis asked the new believer. "Because if you don't, I'm going to send you—and anyone else who phones in—a free copy of the New Testament."

The following morning, President Banzer called David

Farah, a missionary friend of Luis's who served in Bolivia. "I was watching Palau last night," the president said. "If you can get me one million copies of the New Testament, I will pass them on to the Ministry of Education. Instead of having catechism classes, we will have everyone studying the New Testament."

David told Luis what the president had said. They both talked to Chester Schemper. The Bible League took a huge step of faith and accepted the challenge. As a result, since 1975, every primary and secondary school child in Bolivia has studied the New Testament twice a week.

After a crusade in Mexico, Luis returned to Ecuador for a three-week crusade in the capital city of Quito. Five days into the "Quito for Christ '74" crusade, Luis called an executive crusade committee meeting. "The campaign is not going as well as we planned," he said. "People aren't attending the meetings. We don't want to waste anyone's time, so we're canceling the third week."

A chorus of dissent halted the rest of Luis's speech. He mentally staggered from the verbal beating the local committee gave him. By the end of the meeting, they had forced Luis to consent to go the whole way.

I can't believe I gave in to their pressure, Luis thought afterward. But by the end of the crusade he was glad the team had stuck with it. The Bible Society sold out its entire inventory of ten thousand Spanish Bibles and seven thousand New Testaments a week before the crusade ended. As many as ten thousand people attended the meetings some nights, and 3,120 registered their decisions to follow the Lord. In addition, all three weeks of the crusade meetings were broadcast live on the radio to the rest of the continent.

One woman told team member Jim Williams, "I flew

here on a jet from the coastal city of Guayaquil. My psychiatrist told me to come. He said I need to receive Christ."

Jim counseled her that afternoon, she made a public confession of faith at the crusade meeting that evening, and flew home the next day a "new creation" in Christ.

Another decision-maker heard Luis speak at the university, where he held a debate before eight hundred students. This communist leader, impressed by the "guts" it took to do such a thing, decided this Palau fellow deserved another listen. He went to the coliseum that same evening, heard God's Word, received the Lord on the spot, and was saved. "He is having grave persecution problems, as you can imagine," an HCJB missionary wrote to Pat and Luis later that year, "but he is going on with God."

Spain marked the team's first European campaign—the first public evangelistic crusade in Seville's more than two thousand year history. As Luis researched the country's history, he knew the going would be tough. "Eight years ago, Spaniards had no religious freedom," he told Pat. "They changed the laws of the land mainly as a stepping-stone for the country's entry into the European Common Market. Although missionaries there have been preaching the Word for decades, less than five hundred people in a city of 750,000 claim to be born again."

Despite the rocky soil, each night of the crusade more people came to Christ than had received Christ in many years. After the closing night of the five-day crusade, two social police insisted on seeing Luis "alone." Luis sized up the men. The larger of the two could have been an All-Pro defensive lineman. *What now?* he wondered.

"Look," the bigger guy said, "the city of Seville needs

this message very, very much. But the next time you come, we'll get you the bullring. The whole city must hear it. We'll get you the people!"

Luis later admitted, "That's not what I expected to hear."

Although busy ministering in Latin America, Luis felt an equal burden for the people of Europe. *I may have grown up in Argentina*, Luis told himself, *but my family's roots go back to England, France, Germany, Scotland, and Spain. I truly am looking forward to working side by side with Billy Graham and Bishop Festo Kivengere of Uganda for the Eurofest '75 youth congress.*

Through that congress, they hoped to reignite the spark of out-and-out evangelism in a weary land and to challenge eight thousand young people from more than thirty nations to reclaim Europe in Jesus' name.

In the spring of 1975, Pat joined Luis to speak at "minifests" in nine European nations and build momentum for the congress, which would be held in Brussels. Then, three weeks prior to leaving for Eurofest, Luis rushed Pat to the hospital. "She needs emergency surgery," the doctor told Luis. "We must remove her gallbladder and appendix." A successful surgery and fairly rapid recovery meant that Pat and the boys could still accompany Luis to Brussels.

During the congress, Bishop Kivengere and Luis alternated giving the morning Bible study, each being simultaneously translated into thirteen languages. As he prepared for these messages, Luis decided to emphasize the importance of personal holiness and national vision. These two qualities were essential if Europe was going to have a revival that would turn the church and continent upside down, as in the days of John Wesley and George Whitefield.

Partway through the congress, Luis was approached by Harvey Thomas, a member of the Graham team and general secretary for Eurofest. "Luis, we have a problem," he explained. "I originally planned on encouraging all eight thousand youth delegates to attend Sunday morning services at various local churches in Brussels. But while preparing a list of all the area churches, I realized it would be impossible for the small number of churches to accommodate such a huge number of visitors. Instead, I've decided to add a huge Sunday morning worship service to the congress schedule. I know it's last minute, but would you be willing to give the message?"

"Sure," Luis said. He knew that God had used this small favor to help his team break new ground in Western Europe.

As Luis and his family left Brussels, he felt as though his evangelistic team has just received a clear-cut Macedonian call to minister in Europe, like the apostle Paul and his team had nineteen centuries earlier (Acts 16:9–10). But at the same time, there was still a continent to finish reaching back in Latin America.

sixteen

An ambitious strategy kept Luis and the team busy in the fall of 1975. "We'll call it Continente '75," Luis told his team. "We'll broadcast the messages from our crusade in Managua, Nicaragua, and blanket the Americas with the gospel. How? With the help of fifty-six radio stations and more than one hundred television stations from New York to Punta Arenas, Chile, the southernmost city in the world. In one fell swoop, we'll reach an estimated eighty million people in twenty-three countries."

As usual, the city's daily newspapers reported on the twenty-two-day crusade. One morning, Luis picked up a copy of *La Prensa* and read its open attack on the crusade. "They are calling it a 'campaign of conformity,' challenging me to an open debate, and accusing me of being a CIA operative," Luis told Pat later. "Thankfully, the equally secular *Novedades* newspaper defends our character and gives mostly positive front-page coverage to crusade news."

During the final week of the crusade, a woman stopped Luis on his way into Managua's twenty thousand seat National Baseball Stadium. "Gracias, Señor Palau," she managed to say, her voice thick with emotion. "Because you presented the gospel so clearly, my grandson, Danilo, received the Lord several nights ago. The next morning he was so happy. He told me, 'Granny, I've got eternal life.' "

Tears started flowing down her cheeks as she told Luis the rest of the story. "He delivers newspapers, you know. That's what he was doing when. . ." She stopped, unable to continue.

Luis tried to comfort the grandmother and pieced together what he thought must have happened. *Young, excited Danilo probably invited his neighbors to the crusade, and some of them became Christians, too. That's why she's so emotional.*

Her next words shook Luis. "A truck came along. It hit him. I wanted you to know that Danilo's in heaven today." With a hug and another "thank you," she left.

At that night's rally, Luis told Danilo's story just the way his grandmother had told it. Some thirty thousand people gasped as Luis said, "Then a truck came along, and pow!"

The reality of death and the hope of heaven struck home, and many received Jesus Christ as Savior at the end of the service. In addition, millions heard that night's message via satellite and shortwave radio. Little Danilo did not die in vain. All told, more than 5,700 people went forward during the National Stadium meetings.

The spring of 1976 found Luis on the Yucatan Peninsula in Mexico, for eight back-to-back crusades. The mayor of one city told Luis, flat out, "You'll never fill that bullring."

"Mr. Mayor," Luis replied, "we'll fill one half, and God will fill the other half." The last night, some twelve thousand people packed the stands and three-quarters of the Merida bullring grounds—everything except the area reserved for inquirers. More than 430 people made public statements of faith in Jesus Christ that night.

After concluding a five-day crusade in Peru, Luis immediately flew to Bogotá, Colombia. The weekend's evangelistic meetings resulted in decisions to trust Christ from 1,150 of the twenty-four thousand in attendance.

As Luis walked the streets of downtown Bogotá, his heart was filled with thankfulness. He'd never seen so many respond to the gospel outside the context of a full-scale crusade since the first such crusade ten years earlier in this same city. Ten years! Such a short time since Dick Hillis and the OC board had given him the green light to pursue full-time crusade evangelism. *So much has happened during the previous decade. I wonder what's ahead?*

A few weeks later, Luis boarded a plane for his first full-fledged United Kingdom tour. The next two weeks would be spent traveling to thirteen cities in four nations. Luis received a warm welcome everywhere he went on the "Ministry of Thanks" tour. Over and over, Christian leaders invited him to return for major citywide crusades.

The words of a retired missionary to Peru, now living in London, echoed in Luis's ears. "At the turn of the century in this country these prophetic words were spoken: 'The day will come when Third-World missionaries will return to bring the gospel to a post-Christian Britain.' "

So Europe is opening up to me, a Third-World evangelist, after all! Luis thought excitedly. *I'll still evangelize*

Latin America, but I'm convinced that God is calling me to help reevangelize the British Isles, as well. These two goals are complementary, not contradictory. After all, didn't Keith Bentson teach me to pray for the world? And didn't John Wesley once say, "The world is my parish"? Why shouldn't it be my parish, as well, if God so leads?

That summer, the OC board asked Luis to succeed Dick Hillis as president. "Luis, I want to continue working closely and actively with the mission for many more years," Dick said. "I'm only sixty-three, but I feel it is time to hand over the reins."

"But what about my evangelistic work?" Luis asked. "Will my new responsibilities keep me from preaching the gospel?"

After receiving assurances from the OC board, forty-one-year-old Luis accepted the challenge and became the first person from a developing nation ever named president of a U.S.-based missions agency.

I have to keep pressing on, Luis resolved in his mind. *I've seen it happen too often—evangelists burning out after five or ten years, for one reason or another. It's not always pride or sex or money that does them in; more often, they just get tired and give up.* Not that quitting was an option at the moment. Luis smiled as he thought of the many doors God was opening to reach the masses with the claims of Christ.

"So many still need to hear about You, God," he prayed. "Help me to remain faithful to my calling."

seventeen

The man and woman sat side by side without touching. *Together in body, but not in spirit,* Luis thought, watching the two avoid eye contact with him and with each other. *Something is definitely wrong between these two.*

Only a few days earlier, he had accepted the presidency of OC. Now he was in Asunción, Paraguay, for a twelve-day crusade. Besides preaching at the evening evangelistic meetings, Luis spoke at affinity group meetings, offered counsel on live television, and helped at the crusade's family counseling center.

The counseling center was where this couple, both barely thirty, waited in obvious embarrassment. Looking at them, Luis felt a deep sadness. The husband, he learned, was an attorney, the brother of a doctor who served on the crusade committee. "I, um, I've been unfaithful," he told Luis. "It started in my university days. It never meant anything;

fooling around comes naturally to guys." He never thought how his actions might hurt his wife.

The trouble escalated when his wife began taking classes at the university. "His friend," she said, pointing at her husband, "started paying attention to me, sympathizing with me. He would tell me that I was so young and beautiful, that I was wasting my time on a jerk who would cheat on me behind my back."

Luis already knew the outcome. Soon the wife, too, fell into adultery. He could see the suffering on their faces as they said, "We're both ashamed and miserable. We need a solution to our dilemma."

Grabbing his Bible, Luis pointed them to several passages, then he told them, "You need to confess everything to each other—every single thing." Tears began to flow as Luis and the man and the woman knelt together. Impulsively, the couple embraced as they asked God to forgive them. Pulling apart, they then asked each other for forgiveness.

Unashamed, Luis wept as he watched the Lord at work in people's lives. "God, people suffer so much without You in their lives," Luis prayed. "Help me keep alive and burning a compassion for souls. Help me to be ready to weep and cry for the pain through which others are going."

As he drove to the airport at the end of the crusade, Luis reflected on the couple he'd counseled and the 4,900 others who had committed their lives to Christ in Paraguay's capital. Whispering a "thank You, Lord," Luis climbed out of the car and was stopped by a representative of President Alfredo Stroessner. *"Conquistaron!"* the man said. "You conquered!"

Minutes later, as Luis stared out the window of the plane, watching Asunción grow smaller and finally disappear, he thought about his reply to the president's representative: "Actually, the Lord conquered your city and nation for Christ."

If any city needs conquering, it's Rosario, Argentina, Luis said to himself. *That city is about the last place I ever wanted to have a crusade. In fact, if it was up to me, I'd have turned down the invitation.* But Rosario was where he was heading next.

Rosario was a volatile industrial city of more than one million people, with a reputation for gangsterlike bombings, kidnappings, and murders. Spiritually, the city wasn't doing much better. Luis had heard the reports: "Christians are weak and divided; pastors are struggling; churches are languishing." It had taken ninety years of missionary activity to plant forty churches, none of which had more than two hundred members. But team member Ed Silvoso convinced Luis that God was about to turn the city upside down spiritually. And he had envisioned a strategy: the Rosario Plan.

Before the two-week crusade could be held, churches needed to be ready to receive those who made decisions for Jesus Christ. Seminars were held to challenge the pastors to begin training their people in personal evangelism.

"Luis, you wouldn't believe what's happening," Ed reported one day. "Pastors who were complaining about their own apathy toward evangelism and their congregation's lack of enthusiasm are reporting a new vibrancy in their churches. One pastor told me he had written his letter of resignation after months of discouraging church decline. The next thing I know, his congregation has won sixty-five people to Christ and is bursting at the seams."

Thirty-five home-based churches were planted. Then,

during the November 1976 crusade, more than 4,500 people committed their lives to Christ. The two weeks of mass evangelism doubled the number of Christians in Rosario. In addition, more than 110,000 homes throughout the city were visited, and other hundreds of thousands heard the gospel via radio and television.

The Rosario Plan had worked. Three years later, thirty of the thirty-five new churches were thriving, almost doubling what had previously taken almost a century to accomplish.

Back at the office, Luis was fighting an inward battle. "Sometimes the pressure gets to me, Lord," he prayed. "We're preparing for nearly twenty crusades right now. An earthquake in this city, a political upheaval in that city; all of it can affect our upcoming crusade plans. How can I concentrate on writing letters and making phone calls when I read about these crises?"

As he walked over to his desk, Luis noticed a little sign one of the secretaries had placed on it. "For peace of mind, please resign as manager of the universe."

Luis chuckled. "I guess my staff has noticed my tendency, as well, God," he prayed. "I can get too worked up sometimes. It's all too easy to take on burdens no one is asking us to take on, not even You."

An explosive youth crusade in Buenos Aires took Luis back to Argentina in the spring of 1977. Then he took a pilgrimage to Ingeniero-Maschwitz, his family's home prior to their bankruptcy thirty years earlier. "It's always a treat to see how my native country has changed," he told Pat, "and to see whether anyone remembers Luis Palau, the young dreamer who left there in 1960."

His trip home took him to the very chapel that his dad had built and that he had attended during most of his childhood. He had been invited to speak at one of the services.

Luis looked around at the congregation as he waited on the platform. Memories flooded his mind and he tried to swallow the lump in his throat. *That could be me,* he thought as he saw his little nephews wriggling on the hard pews. Emotion overwhelmed Luis when they sang one of his father's favorite hymns, about the joy of bringing other sheep into Christ's fold despite manifold trials. *When my father died, I was still a lost sheep, wandering from God,* Luis thought with tears in his eyes. *He never had the joy of seeing me turn to Christ, let alone watching me follow in his footsteps, leading still other sheep into the family of God.* It was all Luis could do to swallow back his tears and preach his message.

"Thank You, God, for the men You brought into my life after my father's death," Luis prayed afterward. "Men who spiritually nurtured, discipled, trained, and equipped me to serve the King of Kings."

He gave public thanks for these men when he received an honorary doctorate of divinity degree from Talbot Theological Seminary, La Mirada, California, a few days later.

"If they had not come to Argentina," Luis said, "if they had not loved me, if they had not gotten close to me and prayed with me and encouraged me to get on with the Lord's work, I might still be in Argentina, still in that little chapel. . .doing nothing for the Lord."

eighteen

G od has no grandchildren." Luis listened carefully to the elderly gentleman's words. It was the summer of 1977, and Luis had taken a short break from the frenzy of crusade activities in Cardiff, Wales, to speak with retired Welsh missionary David Morris.

"God has no grandchildren," Mr. Morris repeated. "Every generation must experience its own spiritual awakening. I left my land in a state of revival. I returned fifty years later, in my old age, to find it paganized, secularized, and desperately needy of another touch from God."

Paganized is right, Luis silently agreed. *I've never seen anything like it anywhere else in the world.* He thought about the pubs and the sporting events. At every one, the Welsh were guzzling back pint after pint of beer while bellowing gospel hymns. *They absolutely love the old hymns of the faith, but they simply do not know Jesus Christ.*

The crusade helped change that. All told, nearly sixteen

hundred committed their lives to Christ. One young woman who was converted shared what happened with her family. In time, most of them received Christ, as well. One young man was in Cardiff visiting relatives. He heard the crusade needed more ushers, volunteered to help, heard the gospel, and was saved. Later, through his job in television, he helped Luis and the team spread the gospel when they returned to Wales for another crusade twelve years later.

About this time, *Time* magazine reported that Latin America was turning to Christ, with one exception: Uruguay. Once called the "Switzerland of South America," now one-third of the nation claimed "there is no God." So many atheists in one country was unheard of except in the communist world.

"We will face opposition during our crusades here," Luis said to himself when he arrived in Montevideo, Uruguay's capital. "But God can work that to His advantage. His truth can break down the atheistic and materialistic philosophies that have pervaded the entire country."

From Montevideo, Luis traveled west, then south, then east, then north for six back-to-back crusades along Uruguay's border. Flying from city to city was out of the question, so Luis and his team members bounced along the sixteen hundred miles of dusty roads (sometimes overrun by herds of cattle) in an assortment of older vehicles (some that required more oil than gas) to present the gospel to more than one hundred thousand men, women, and young people. When Luis heard the report that more than 8,100 Uruguayans had come to faith in Christ during the crusade meetings, his exhaustion melted away. *What a response to the gospel*, he said to himself. *I like preaching to atheists!*

He remembered one call he had received during one of

143

their live counseling television programs. A woman bluntly told him, "I'm an atheist."

"So, why are you calling me, then?" he asked.

"I want you to convince me, Palau. Sell me on God, please!"

Another woman turned on her television and heard Luis talking about family problems. Nancy couldn't stop watching. Her marriage was ending in divorce. She and her husband, Bario, hadn't slept in the same bed in five years. They wouldn't even eat together. When the program ended, Nancy cried out, "Lord, if it's true that You exist, why are these things happening to me?"

That night, Nancy told Bario that she was going to-morrow to the Luis Palau crusade at the Palacio Penarol Stadium in Montevideo. Then she shuddered. *I talked to Bario*, she realized. *We haven't spoken in ages*. Bario and Nancy both ended up going to the crusade and committing their lives and marriage to Christ.

"From that moment our lives have changed completely," Nancy told Luis later. "Every day we are surprised at how much we learn. We pray together, we share things together. . . . People say we aren't the same." Within five months Nancy and Bario had led thirty-five people to Jesus!

After Uruguay, Luis flew to OC headquarters in California. Two years had passed since he had accepted the presidency; now it was time to meet with the board of directors and review the situation.

Luis looked at the faces around the table. He had grown to love and respect these men on the OC board. Telling them his decision would be hard. He stood, took a deep breath, then began: "I've spent a lot of time in thought and in prayer," he said. "I love OC and owe such a great debt to Dick Hillis, but I feel compelled to ask you to free me from my responsibilities as president. In many ways, it's becoming impossible to manage my own thirty-member evangelistic team and give OC the leadership it needs and deserves."

Luis sat again. As he listened to the discussion, he knew the board had come to the same conclusion. "Luis, you have our full blessing," they told him.

It was official. On October 1, 1978, the Luis Palau Evangelistic Association (LPEA) became a separate missions organization with headquarters in Portland, Oregon. Soon, Luis and his family would come to live in Portland, as well.

A few weeks later, Luis left for Bolivia, a bit concerned about the responsibilities now facing him as head of LPEA. But the national revival that occurred in Bolivia immediately stopped his second-guessing.

"The stadium is so packed that La Paz police have to close the gates each night, Luis," his team members told him. "Hundreds of would-be crusade-goers are being turned away."

"Then let's hold two services," Luis replied.

They scheduled an afternoon and an evening service for both Saturday and Sunday. Still, the lines of people waiting to enter the stadium stretched for blocks.

Our Bolivia crusade four years ago was tremendous, Luis thought on Sunday night. *We reaped a plentiful harvest. But nothing could have prepared me for this. What a revival! And we still have two more cities to go. God, let this movement of the Spirit continue.*

The Lord continued to amaze Luis. In Santa Cruz and Cochabamba, the three weeks of meetings broke almost every crusade record the team had ever set with 180,000 in attendance and 18,916 decisions for Christ.

Luis let his mind drift back several weeks, back to a midmorning press conference in a La Paz hotel room. The journalists had thrown him question after question, scratching down his answers on their notepads. Hearing the door open, Luis had looked over and seen a little girl slip into the room.

That's the daughter of the hotel elevator operator, Luis had realized. *What could she possibly want?*

He had reached for a copy of one of his books, pulled out a pen and autographed it. With a whispered, "The Lord bless you, sweetheart," Luis had smiled and handed the book to the eleven-year-old. But the little girl had shrugged away his offer.

"Mr. Palau, what I really wanted to ask you was how I could receive Jesus in my heart. You see, last night I watched you counsel people on national television. Remember when you spoke to that high school student and led him to Christ? That's what I want to do. I want to receive Him, too."

Luis chuckled as he remembered how they had shooed the newsmen out of the room. Publicity was necessary and fine, but their questions could wait until another time. Like 2 Corinthians 6:2 says, "Now is the day of salvation" —whether it's an eleven-year-old girl or the president of a nation.

Even now, he got excited when he thought about the Presidential Prayer Breakfast with Bolivia's new president, General Juan Pereda Asbun, and many other high-ranking leaders. After his twenty-minute address, Luis listened as President Pereda stood up and reaffirmed the importance of setting "personal and national spiritual priorities" and publicly endorsed the Bolivia crusades.

Later Luis met Pereda in his presidential office. As they talked, Luis asked the president about his own relationship with Jesus and explained the way to find forgiveness. Right there, President Pereda bowed his head and gave his life to Christ.

Never before have we seen so many from every walk of life give their lives to the Lord, Luis thought. *Having such a successful crusade after launching out on our own is a godsend. In my heart, I feel God is reaffirming His call on my life and His blessing on our team.*

nineteen

They're trying to shout me down, Luis thought in surprise. His first lecture at the University of Sydney
had been going well, until now. Slightly rattled, Luis
ignored the group of Marxist-Leninists and continued
speaking to the eight hundred students on the mall who
were enjoying that spring day in 1979.

"Former U.S. Secretary of State Henry Kissinger
observed that there are no more than twenty-four free
nations left in the world," Luis told the students. "One
striking characteristic of those twenty-four nations is that
all have been profoundly influenced by evangelistic awak-
enings within the past two or three centuries. You are reap-
ing the benefits of living in a nation that has been blessed
because of its Christian roots.

"Even if a nation is now pagan and in need of massive
change, there is only one revolution that works, and that's
the revolution in the heart through faith in Jesus Christ."

At this statement, one Marxist agitator pointed his finger at Luis and shouted obscenities. *He looks like a young Fidel Castro,* Luis thought, then tried to intelligently debate him. The only response was more swear words. "Those vile words you're shouting at me don't prove anything," Luis told the angry young man, "except that you have no basis for your beliefs." Duly silenced, the man skulked away and Luis finished speaking.

Later that day, Luis told his team members, "Speaking to university students on their turf is always a bit unnerving. But when those communist radicals tried to shout me down, I admit I started thinking about canceling my other upcoming university lectures."

There were no cancellations, however. Luis kept preaching the Word at four other universities in Australia, at evening crusade meetings at the Newcastle Showgrounds, and through media interviews.

Later that spring, Luis and the team arrived in Scotland for a crusade. As they drove to Aberdeen, Luis kept looking out the window at the beautiful valleys lush with vegetation and the empty, dilapidated churches long ago boarded up. *Everywhere I look, Scots are rejecting empty ritual and dead religion,* Luis said to himself. *My heart aches when I think of the very few who have experienced the reality of the resurrected, living Lord Jesus Christ.* Then his thoughts turned to prayer: "Lord, let Your Spirit work again in the land where men of God such as John Knox, Robert Murray M'Cheyne, and Andrew Bonar once saw revival and the salvation of thousands of souls. Start with our crusade in Aberdeen."

Scots, however, were skeptical about a revival ever happening again in their country. "Aren't you trying to flog a dead horse?" one British Broadcasting Corporation news-man asked Luis. Another journalist asked Luis, "Why are you wasting your time on a post-Christian society?"

"I don't believe there is any such thing as a post-Christian society," Luis replied. "Either a person is or isn't a Christian. One generation may reject the gospel for itself, but each new generation has the opportunity to make its own choice. I cannot accept that a society can exist where the gospel is no longer relevant."

By the crusade's end, Luis had watched hundreds of people come to Christ, including nearly one thousand teenagers, and had accepted an invitation from churches in half a dozen other parts of Scotland to return the next year for more evangelistic rallies and crusades. But first, it was time to go home and see his family. He returned in time to hear some distressing news from one of his sons.

"Kevin, I just heard about the sixteen-year-old boy from your school," Luis said to his son. "You knew him, right?"

"Yes," Kevin replied. "Dad, I just can't believe he committed suicide. He had everything going for him. He did fine in school and was involved in lots of activities. His family was wealthy. They went on great vacations and even had horses. Nobody could have guessed he would put a gun to his head and shoot himself."

"Did he show any signs of unusual stress?"

"No, Dad. I saw him just three hours before it happened. But about an hour after he got home from school, he called some guys and told them he was going to kill himself."

"What did they do?" Luis asked. "What did they say to him?"

"The guys didn't believe him," Kevin said. "He hadn't seemed upset, so they thought he was joking."

Luis offered up a quick, silent prayer for the boy's family, then turned to comfort his hurting boy. That evening, Luis took Kevin and Keith to see a film on death and dying at their local high school. Afterward, they discussed the movie.

"Boys, what do you think?" Luis asked. "Do the deceased just become a 'memory,' as the film suggests?"

"No, Dad," they replied, "that's not what the Bible teaches."

"That's right," Luis said. "That's a romantic idea without any basis in reality. The Bible, in Hebrews 9:27, teaches us that 'man is destined to die once, and after that to face judgment.' By trusting in Jesus Christ, we can have our sins forgiven and know we're going to heaven."

"I'm so glad that both Kevin and Keith know the Lord," Luis told Pat after the boys went to bed. "But I long to see them want to know God more."

"I do too, Luis," she replied. "Sometimes I wonder if they are becoming overly attracted by what the world has to offer."

Side by side, on their knees, Luis and Pat took their concerns about their sons to the feet of Jesus.

That fall, Luis was the main speaker at the second Latin American Conference on Evangelism in Lima, Peru. Then he finished off the year with a crusade in Caracas, Venezuela.

"The 1970s are drawing to a close," Luis told his team back at the office. "Have we accomplished our goal of saturating Latin America with the gospel? In many ways, yes. We have ministered in many of the capitals and other leading cities across the continent. We have broadcast the gospel through television and radio to at least one out of every three Spanish-speaking people in the world. We have distributed many millions of evangelistic booklets and tracts.

"But the same doors that have been open for the gospel the past decade have also remained open for the Marxists and other enemies of the gospel. The battle for the heart and soul of Latin America is far from over! Let us enter the 1980s more committed than ever to continue to evangelize the masses all across Latin America."

At the same time, Luis knew that he needed to continue preaching the Word whenever and wherever the Lord gave him an opportunity. That's why he rang in the new decade in England, speaking at fifteen youth rallies in ten cities in two weeks. More than 2,700 people registered commitments to Jesus Christ.

Often Luis found himself discussing the state of the church with Christian leaders.

"Just a year ago, the BBC was calling Britain a post-Christian society," they would say. "What do you think?"

"God has no grandchildren," Luis would answer, repeating what he had learned from Welsh missionary David Morris three years earlier. "A generation ago, Britain was alive to God. Now, churches by the hundreds are closing, often being converted into mosques or Hindu temples. British companies are shipping hundreds of tons of church furnishings to America, Japan, and Western Europe for auction to antique dealers. But no society is post-Christian. There's hope. Revival can happen."

Sadly, Luis discovered that some of Britain's most prominent church leaders disagreed, going on record saying, "There's nothing we can do to reverse such dismal trends."

If it takes a third-generation, transplanted European who was born in the Third World and who now claims American citizenship to help turn the tide in Britain, Luis decided, *so be it.*

That spring, Luis returned to Britain for a six-city tour of Scotland. Anticipating some opposition from the media, government officials, or antireligious groups, Luis was quite surprised when the attack came from inside the church. In a private meeting, a dozen Scottish ministers expressed their disapproval with "organized mass evangelistic efforts," and at least half admitted they did not accept the Bible as the trustworthy Word of God.

"Is it any wonder their churches are faltering and failing?" Luis asked himself. "Who wants to listen to ministers who readily dismiss portions of Scripture? Since when did God ask for anyone's help to make His Book more politically correct?"

Despite the ministers' attitudes, people turned out for the evangelistic rallies and crusades by the droves. Two thousand committed their lives to Jesus Christ in a week and a half.

Just as Luis and Pat prepared to leave Scotland, they found themselves confronted with the biggest challenge of their lives. Pat discovered a lump in one breast. They rushed home and to their doctor. Medical tests showed that she might have cancer. The doctor would have to do a biopsy. Waiting in the doctor's office a few days later, Luis and Pat steeled themselves for the verdict. Then came the awful words: "The tumor is malignant and radical surgery must be performed immediately. We can't delay." Surgery was scheduled for the following Monday.

twenty

L uis slipped down the stairs into the basement of his house. He headed to his office. What had he said to Pat on the ride back from the doctor's office? He couldn't remember much of anything after the words *tumor, malignant,* and *surgery.*

He put his head in his hands. *Somehow I have to come to grips with this terrible blow,* he told himself as a hundred emotions welled up inside him. Tears fell down his face, one after another. He hurt inside in a way he never knew he could. *This is the sort of thing that happens to other people, but not to my wife. Not to Pat.*

Then the sounds of a favorite hymn broke into his thoughts. *Where is the music coming from?* Luis wondered. *Our four boys are all at school. No one is in the house except Pat and me.* As he listened, realization slowly dawned on him. *It's Pat. She's playing the piano and singing "How Firm a Foundation."*

He silently sang the words of the second verse as Pat
continued to play:

"Fear not, I am with thee; O be not dismayed,
"For I am thy God, and will still give thee aid;
"I'll strengthen thee, help thee, and cause thee
    to stand,
"Upheld by My righteous, omnipotent hand."

"Thank You, God, for the reminder," Luis said out loud.
"The bottom may be falling out of our lives. That's all the
more reason to place our security and strength in You
alone. You will see us through these deep waters, too."

That afternoon, Luis broke the news to their sons. None
of them said anything. They just looked at their dad. Then
Steve, the youngest of the four and only eleven years old at
the time, blurted out, "But, Daddy, people die from cancer!"

"That's true, but we believe God is going to make
Mommy better again," Luis said. "She won't be feeling
very well for a long time, so that will mean some changes
around here, for all of us. You guys are going to have to
learn to take care of yourselves, and to help Mommy every
way you can."

While Pat was recuperating at home after surgery, she
and Luis began discussing his immediate ministry plans.
"The first concern is our crusade in Los Angeles," Luis
said. "We've been preparing for this—our first full-scale
Spanish-language crusade here in America—for two years.
The publicity is all out. But we can cancel the whole thing,
even though it's last-minute."

"No, Luis, I think you should go," Pat said. "Kevin and
Keith are seventeen years old. They can stay home to help

155

take care of me."

"And I can take the two younger boys with me. They're already used to the idea of traveling with me from time to time, and the trip can help soothe their fears."

Pat started chemotherapy treatment, at first every week, then every other week when she got too sick. Luis and Pat knew the odds for survival and other cancer statistics, but they determined from the beginning not to play the "What if?" game.

"My life is in God's hands," Pat said again and again. "I'm not going to shake my fist in God's face, even if the so-called experts tell me to 'vent my feelings.' God knows what He is doing, and He has given us a doctor who knows what he's doing also."

When the mail arrived, Luis would sort through it. Letters of encouragement went straight to Pat. The least helpful articles and books—the last thing Pat needed at that point—were set aside. One time, Luis interrupted one woman's monologue to say, "Look, lady, you can cut people's hair, but you are not going to give us medical advice!"

What Pat found she needed and so appreciated were the calls and visits of friends who listened and shared an appropriate verse of Scripture with her. Jeremiah 29:11 became a favorite for both Pat and Luis: " 'I know the plans I have for you,' " declares the LORD, " 'plans to prosper you and not to harm you, plans to give you hope and a future.' "

After returning from the crusade in Los Angeles, Luis told his wife, "The Lord used this crusade, Pat. Nearly two thousand people committed their lives to the Lord. One fourteen-year-old gang member had just been treated at a hospital for gunshot and knife wounds, and then he decided to come to the meeting where he made a decision for Christ."

Their conversation soon turned to what should be done about Luis's upcoming schedule. Some hard decisions had to be made. They decided to cancel a trip in June to the Congress on World Evangelization in Pattaya, Thailand, where Luis was scheduled to be one of the main speakers.

Luis did travel that fall to South America for crusades in five cities and in Guayaquil, Ecuador, where his crusade messages were broadcast by HCJB Radio to at least ten nations. His call-in counseling television program was broadcast live for twelve nights to the entire nation and to much of neighboring Colombia and Peru, as well.

The record books will show that more than 2,800 made decisions for Christ during the Guayaquil crusade meetings, Luis told himself later, *but only eternity will reveal how many were converted through television and radio. I know at least 180 people called to complain when my nightly radio broadcasts stopped.*

Suddenly he had an idea. With Pat so sick, why not make more extensive use of the media this next year? The more he thought and prayed about it, the more sense it made. Finally Luis broached the subject with his team, who readily agreed. But what region should be the target for this all-out evangelistic media blitz? A bit more discussion yielded the answer: Central America, which was reeling from recent guerrilla attacks and civil war. They would broadcast from Guatemala, where they had already seen so much fruit and where they had been invited to return in two years for the centennial celebration of the gospel coming to that nation.

But besides Pat's ongoing battle with cancer, Luis now had other reasons to curtail his crusade travels: His two oldest boys were definitely becoming too interested in the things of this earth. He and Pat felt that Kevin and Keith were spending too much time listening to secular rock music, and Pat and Luis were concerned about the influence of some of the twins' friends. During one discussion, Pat said bluntly, "If you don't stay home, Luis, these boys will go straight into the world."

Luis panicked. "If any of my sons walked away from the Lord, my heart would break."

They decided to give it six months before taking any drastic steps. "If we see no change in Kevin and Keith," Luis said, "I'll drop all of my crusade commitments and stay home to be with them. That's the way it has to be."

Soon after that, Kevin and Keith attended a Christian concert in town. Singer Keith Green helped put them back on track. Then, at a retreat, both of them consecrated their lives to God and applied to attend Wheaton College, a Christian school in Illinois.

Pat and Luis could now rest easy. In gratitude they prayed, "Thank You, Lord. We can carry on." Not that their struggles were over, by any means.

twenty-one

Five weeks is a long time to be away from those you love. For Luis, those five weeks in 1981 seemed like a lifetime. Pat still fought her battle with cancer, enduring grueling chemotherapy treatments that left her weak and weary, sick and in pain.

If I could, I would be at home right now, instead of in Scotland for weeks on end, Luis thought. *But like Pat said, Glasgow needs me more than she does right now. Not that I'm anything special, but this crusade is the culmination of our strategy to reevangelize this nation. And you can't make a national impact overnight.*

On the opening Sunday of the campaign, Luis told the Scots gathered in Kelvin Hall, "It's either back to the Bible or back to the jungle," echoing something Billy Graham had once said.

The following morning, when Luis picked up a copy of the *Glasgow Herald,* he saw his remark on the front page.

Throughout the morning and afternoon, he heard mention of it again and again. For days, it was the topic of discussion and debate on television, radio, and the editorial pages of several newspapers. Luis could hardly believe the controversy created by his statement, but he determined to use all the attention to help the Scots see their need for God.

After the thirty-six-day crusade was completed, Luis asked himself, "Was it worth it, slugging it out day in and day out for five straight weeks? Definitely."

He was reminded of a teenage girl who lived about fifteen miles from Kelvin Hall. She had attended the team's friendship evangelism training and had taken up the challenge to regularly pray by name for five or ten unsaved friends or family members. Then she invited all of them to the crusade meetings. She decided to rent a bus, convinced that she could fill it with friends. But when she invited her friends, not one accepted. Upset, she called the crusade prayer committee and asked them to intercede. Then she went back to her friends and persuaded thirty-eight of them to attend the crusade with her. At Kelvin Hall, every single one of her friends went forward to receive Christ! Luis loved seeing someone so young step out in complete faith to help people meet Jesus Christ. All told, more than 5,325 people publicly gave their lives to the Lord during the Glasgow crusade.

On the flight home, Luis began to think about the San Diego campaign coming up that summer. He was still not sure about accepting that invitation. The crusade would be his first full-scale English-language event in the United States. But ever since he had come to this country, he had felt God telling him that he should pour himself into crusade evangelism overseas until Billy Graham started to slow down. *It's been twenty years, and Billy is still going as strong as ever. Will God ever clearly show me that I can minister in the United States? Is my dream of evangelizing America's cities always going to be only a dream?*

Luis soon regretted his impatient decision to preach in San Diego. Oh, Pat didn't mind him leaving for a week and a half. In fact, she joined him to speak one morning to a group of two thousand women about her struggles with cancer and the need to trust Jesus Christ to stand strong through life's storms. Luis also rejoiced that through the crusade more than twelve hundred people committed their lives to Jesus Christ. Still he prayed afterward, "God, I feel I somehow disobeyed You. It's true You are opening the door for us to expand our ministry in the United States, but now I understand that the door will open slowly, according to Your schedule, not mine."

Back home, Luis received a phone call. "Do you remember Mandy?" the person asked him.

How could I forget? Luis thought. He had met thirteen-year-old Mandy three years earlier at a youth rally at a church in Richmond, outside London. She had spent several minutes talking with him about her eternal destiny. Mandy had told Luis that her father, a famous London jazz musician, and her mother, a well-known British actress, were divorced. They had never attended church, had never talked about God, and didn't even own a Bible. Mandy said she had never heard about Jesus Christ until that night when Luis spoke about Him. But when she learned that Jesus died for her sins on a Roman cross, rose again, and was coming back to take all those who believed in Him to heaven, she had prayed and invited Jesus into her heart.

As they had neared the end of their discussion, Luis

had shown her what Jesus says to all believers in John 10:28: "I give them eternal life, and they shall never perish; no one can snatch them out of my hand." He clearly remembered Mandy's reply. She had said, "That's what I've got." Smiling at the memory, Luis asked the caller about the girl.

"Three days before Mandy turned sixteen, she went on a date," the caller told Luis. "It had begun to drizzle, and the car swerved out of control and crashed. Mandy's date was thrown clear of the convertible and was uninjured. But Mandy died instantly."

Later, Luis talked with Mandy's parents, who asked him to "give the sermon" at her funeral service, because they said, "Mandy talked about nothing more than Jesus, Luis Palau, and going to heaven."

On the day of the funeral, the church was filled with famous personalities, all of whom had a view of the casket that contained Mandy's body.

"Ladies and gentlemen," Luis said to these famous people, "what you see in the casket is not Mandy. It is Mandy's body, but the real Mandy is not here. Mandy is in heaven with Jesus Christ, because the Bible says, 'Away from the body and at home with the Lord' (2 Corinthians 5:8).

"We're going to bury Mandy's body this afternoon," Luis continued. "But the Bible says that the body is just the house of the soul and spirit—the essence of who we really are. Because Mandy had eternal life, she went straight to heaven when she died. Although her body will stay here, her soul and spirit went immediately to be with the Lord."

Afterward, Luis talked with Mandy's mother. "I wish to God I had what Mandy had," she told Luis. With his heart breaking, Luis watched her end their conversation

162

and walk away still in despair, still without Christ.

That fall, Kevin and Keith left for Illinois and their first semester at Wheaton College. They returned home for the holidays a few days after a bone scan revealed Pat had no signs of cancer anywhere. The usual celebrations for Christmas and New Year's became even more special—the family was back together again and Pat's cancer was gone.

One evening, the family gathered for prayer to thank the Lord for sparing Pat's life. As they talked to God, Luis silently added his thanks for using that time of adversity to give Pat a wider platform for ministry. Suddenly, editors were asking her for articles. She started receiving more invitations to speak at women's conferences and evangelistic meetings. Crusade committees wanted her to come and share her testimony. "God, You are the Master Planner," Luis prayed. "With Kevin and Keith in college, and Andrew and Steve growing more independent, the timing couldn't have been better."

"This year, 1982, we have seven crusades scheduled on four continents," Luis told his team members. "Not since 1969 have we attempted so many crusades in such a short period of time."

The first stop was the University of Wisconsin in Madison that February. Many Christian organizations had helped open the campus to spiritual issues. When talking with their student leaders, Luis was astounded to learn that most came from broken homes or homes where the parents didn't personally know God. One night at a rally, Luis said, "There was a time when parents prayed for their children. Now children pray for their parents."

After the meeting a man walked up to Luis, the smell

of alcohol accompanying him. "Luis," he said, "I am one of those parents being prayed for by my children."

As Luis watched the man step carefully away, he thought, *I am more convinced than ever that we need to evangelize this land.*

From Wisconsin, it was on to Newcastle, Australia, for their second crusade in the city in three years. Having completed her final chemotherapy treatment, Pat was able to join Luis for the closing week of the Newcastle crusade. Through the crusade meetings, media interviews, and live television counseling, the city opened up to the gospel in an amazing way. "If it were humanly possible, I'd love to go back to every city where we've had a crusade," Luis told Pat afterward. "We often see two, three, even four times as much fruit."

After a short crusade in Bellingham, Washington, Luis flew to Helsinki, Finland, for the first united evangelistic crusade in that country since the Reformation and the team's first full-fledged crusade outside the English- and Spanish-speaking worlds.

"I've translated for others and I've even had people translate for me before," Luis told one of his team members, "but never all day long, all week long, for every single event. I can't even ask a waitress for a cup of coffee without someone else's help."

The chuckles his comment received made Luis smile, too. *It is rather amusing,* he thought. *But I've also been humbled by it, to see how the Holy Spirit so intricately weaves my words with my translator's as we proclaim the gospel in one language and then another.*

From Finland, Luis knew he would be flying to Asunción, Paraguay; to Leeds, England; then to Guatemala City. Feeling dead tired just thinking about his fast-paced schedule and the many miles he had to travel, Luis was tempted to complain. That's when he received a not-so-gentle reminder from God. It was almost as if the voice of the Lord said, *"Oh, you are tired, are you? Do you want Me to take away this opportunity and that opportunity and trim back your crusade schedule and let you start twiddling your thumbs waiting for something to do? Just give Me the word."*

In a bit of a panic, Luis began to pray. "No, Lord, forgive me for even thinking about complaining. I love to be Your ambassador, and I'm ready for my next assignment."

God doesn't owe me anything, Luis realized. *He's not obligated to keep using me. My ministry could be over in a minute if the Lord so chooses. Everything I do and everything I am is thanks to His mercy and grace. Like John Wesley, George Whitefield, Charles Finney, D. L. Moody, Billy Graham, and others before me, I want to be found faithful to Christ to the end.*

He then recalled a conversation he'd had with a youth evangelist several months before at a Christian conference. "Luis, you may hear one of these days about a teenage girl that goes around saying I had a love affair with her," the man said. "Don't believe a word of it."

"What do you mean?" Luis asked. "Why would she say something like that about you? Is something going on that you need to talk about?"

"Forget it," he said coldly. "I wish I hadn't mentioned it."

Luis remembered the shock and grief he had felt when he discovered this man with whom he had worked in the past had left his wife, his children, and his ministry. He kept the secret for years: feeding a pornography addiction while preaching up a storm against immorality. Then, the inevitable happened. He started committing adultery. He had affairs going in city after city. When the truth finally came out, he had walked out on his family.

Again, Luis began to pray, "Lord, You have kept us from dishonoring Your name all these years. Please keep us until the end of the road, faithful, holy, fruitful for Your glory."

In his heart, Luis wanted to win this fallen brother back to God. But later attempts failed. Although sorry for all the troubles he had brought upon himself, the man refused to repent of his wicked ways and get back to God. He did try to get back into the ministry as if nothing had happened, but he was finished. You can't play games with God like that.

During this same period, several other well-known Christian leaders fell into rather despicable sins. *It seems like an epidemic,* Luis said to himself. *What's going on? If this could happen to this one and that one and this other one it could happen to me.*

Luis went to Dick Hillis, who had been walking with the Lord for sixty-some years. "Why are all these guys falling away?" Luis asked.

Dick thought and thought about it. Finally, he told Luis, "I think it's because they were reading a lot of books about the Bible, but not the Bible itself."

Luis pondered Dick's words, then came to the conclusion that nothing can take the place of God's Word, not even the best biblical commentaries. An evangelist or preacher or teacher needs to do his homework. He needs to read widely and deeply. But even Billy Graham once admitted that if he could do it all over again, he would have read fewer books and spent even more time reading the Book. Saturating himself with Scripture became Luis's goal, as well. "I may have been studying the Scriptures daily all my adult life," he told himself, "but that is no excuse to slack off now!"

twenty-two

His gaze roamed over the crowded stadium as he gave the invitation. *Lord, it's our last night in Paraguay,* Luis prayed silently as he spoke. *So many still need to be converted. Work in the lives of that distraught couple sitting off to my left, whose eyes are full of tears. Open the hearts of the group of young people sitting directly in front of me toward the back. Help the leaders of this city, those standing behind me on the platform, to realize they need Christ just as much as anyone else this evening.*

Stepping back from the microphone, Luis watched as waves of people left their seats and walked forward. On the opening Sunday, they had set a team record for the most people counseled in a single meeting. What would God do tonight?

"It's a brand-new record, Luis," one team member told him. "An astounding 1,690 people came forward to give their lives to the Lord. That means more than 10,550 people registered public commitments to Christ during our crusade here."

The team felt little spiritual resistance to proclaiming the gospel in Paraguay, but they found exactly the opposite to be true in Leeds, England, a few weeks later.

"I've never seen such spiritual warfare in all my life," Luis told his team members.

They nodded, remembering how members of a satanic group had heckled Luis whenever he read from the Bible or mentioned the blood of Jesus Christ. Several of the occultists had rushed past security guards and stormed the platform as he read from Ephesians 6. Other cultic groups had threatened to burn down the big-top tent where the crusade meetings were held.

"We've fought an all-out battle for the souls of men and women, youth and children," Luis continued, "but the Lord gave us the victory, drawing nearly 1,000 to Himself. Now, on to Guatemala!"

A few months earlier, Guatemala had experienced such political upheaval that Luis and the team wondered if they would have to cancel the crusade. Weeks passed before the word came from Central American field director Benjamin Orozco: "Luis, the crusade can proceed as planned. Guatemala is experiencing relative peace."

So off they went for the week-long crusade. When Luis woke on Thanksgiving Sunday, he sensed the excitement surrounding the city. Today, Christians from all across Guatemala would celebrate the coming of the gospel to their nation one hundred years ago, and he would have the privilege of speaking to them.

"They're leaving their houses right now," Luis reflected. "So many Christians from all across the country gathering on the street corners. Then when the sun rises, they will march in columns down the city's widest avenues toward Campo Marte."

But nothing could have prepared Luis for what was about to happen. Tens of thousands, then soon hundreds of thousands of people began filling the massive empty military parade ground. Military helicopters flew overhead, trying to estimate the crowd's size. . .first five hundred thousand, then six hundred thousand, finally seven hundred thousand people!

The transistor radios many in the crowd carried buzzed and popped as they tuned into one of the dozen radio stations that broadcast the event live. Now this vast sea of people could sing together and hear the speakers without missing one word.

In the middle of the ceremony, Luis watched as several Chevrolet Suburbans slowly drove into the mass of people, edging them out of their path. *I wonder what's going on?* Luis asked himself as the vehicles finally maneuvered their way to the platform. Then, President Efrain Rios Montt, an outspoken evangelical, climbed out of one of the Suburbans, walked to the podium, and addressed the crowd.

Finally, the time came for Luis to speak. As usual, he gave an invitation for people to make a decision for Christ. "There's no way we can ask people to come forward in a crowd of this size," Luis said to himself. "We'll have to leave the results in God's capable hands."

"Why, Luis?" several people asked him after hearing how he had preached to the largest gathering of Christians in Latin America's history. "After preaching to seven hundred thousand in Guatemala City, why are you having a crusade in Hermosillo, Mexico?"

"Simply put, we go where the Spirit leads," Luis replied. "The crusade is going to be small, that's true. Evangelicals make up less than one percent of the population, and the gym where I'll be speaking each night only holds a maximum of five thousand people. Are we to wait and accept only the biggest and best possible crusade invitations? That's absurd. Our team's conviction is that we must make the most of every year the Lord gives us."

A crusade in Hermosillo may have defied natural logic, but the Lord blessed the team's efforts there. People filled the gymnasium, then overflowed outside the building, where they listened to the service over loudspeakers. All told, 3,450 people (including the city's mayor) received Jesus Christ or rededicated their lives to the Lord. The Christian population of Hermosillo doubled in a week!

Luis boarded a plane for London. In the fall of 1983, he had preached at nine regional crusades throughout that city. Now, six months later, he was returning for an even more ambitious seven-week crusade. They were calling it Mission to London.

Soon after arriving, a dinner party was held as a welcome for Mission to London. Luis found his seat beside a member of the royal family. After greeting him, the princess said politely, "Dr. Palau, I'm going to talk to this gentleman for twenty minutes, then I will talk to you. Is that all right?"

"Yes, Your Royal Highness," Luis said. Almost exactly twenty minutes later, the princess turned back to him.

"Dr. Palau, I have wanted to talk to an evangelist for years and years," she began, her face as earnest as her words. "I have a question. Do you have assurance of eternal life? And, if you do, how did you come about it? And, if one wanted to have this same assurance, how would one get it? Can you help me?"

"Yes, ma'am, I can help you," Luis said, realizing at the same time that he had but a few minutes to answer her questions. Luis quickly presented the gospel, then quoted 1 John 5:11–12, " 'God has given us eternal life, and this life is in his Son. He who has the Son has life; he who does not have the Son of God does not have life.' "

"But how do I get the Son of God if I want life?" she asked.

"Ma'am, the Bible says in John 1:12, 'Yet to all who received him, to those who believed in his name, he gave the right to become children of God.' "

"But, Dr. Palau," she asked earnestly, "how do I receive Him into my heart? What do I have to do?"

"Your Highness, you pray a simple prayer and invite Jesus into your heart. Jesus says in Revelation 3:20, 'I stand at the door and knock. If anyone hears my voice and opens the door, I will come in and eat with him, and he with me.' It would be as if I were to go to the palace this afternoon and knock on the door. You might look out the window and say to your husband, 'Oh dear, it's Palau. What are we going to do? He talks too much. Do we let him in or not?' "

Luis smiled, then continued, "If you want me to come into your home, all you have to do is send one of the guards to open the door and say, 'Come in, Luis, take a seat. What would you like to drink?' And I will come into your house and visit with you."

The princess, although having listened intently, still looked perplexed. Finally she asked, "But how do I open the door of my heart?"

Luis slowly put his hand in his pocket and pulled out a copy of the Four Spiritual Laws. Deciding that leading her in prayer right there wouldn't be a good idea, he handed her the booklet and said, "Your Highness, put this in your purse, and tonight when you get to the palace, explain to your husband what I have told you now. Then get on your knees beside your bed, and together pray the prayer in this booklet, inviting Jesus into your hearts."

The princess smiled in gratitude. "Thank you. I have waited all of my life to know how to have eternal life." Later that night at home, she opened her heart to Christ.

The meetings began at Queen's Park Rangers (QPR) Stadium. For six weeks, night after night, Luis proclaimed the gospel. People of every creed, color, religious background, and walk of life trusted Jesus Christ—a top rock star, a famous actress, a disillusioned policeman, a car dealer, a truck driver, the official crusade photographer, a gentleman whose wife had prayed for his salvation for twenty-one years, twenty-five boys from a British boarding school, a young gang member who had helped disrupt the meeting earlier that same evening, a runaway teenager, and more than a few religious ministers.

By the final night, cumulative attendance for Mission to London had topped 518,000 and more than 28,000 had made public commitments to Jesus Christ. Then the last week of June, Luis's crusade messages were broadcast to all fifty nations of the British Commonwealth.

Tomorrow, I leave London, Luis thought, then chuckled as he remembered the "Luis, go home!" graffiti that had been appearing around the city. *Some people may have not wanted me here, but I praise God that He allowed me to come. I feel like cheering because so many came to Christ. I guess I'm in good company. Jesus says there's rejoicing in heaven when even one person repents (Luke 15). What a celebration there must be when thousands turn to the Lord during a crusade!*

twenty-three

Some questioned the wisdom of the team's decision. Sometimes Luis questioned it himself. Should they really go to Peru for a crusade that fall when guerrillas were on the rampage? He had read the news. Maoist Sendero Luminoso (Shining Path) guerrillas wanted to create a new society and had wiped out entire villages in the process. Some of the country's leaders had been executed, and more than forty pastors and four hundred other believers had been killed in the bloody wake of the Shining Path.

Now the Shining Path guerrillas had become even more violent, and Americans were the target. They had even attacked the American Embassy. It was all-out war. Luis and Pat discussed it at length. As an American evangelist, should he still risk going for two-and-a-half weeks of evangelism in two of Peru's largest cities? Both of them stood firm. Luis would go, come what may.

The first crusade in the city of Arequipa, Peru, concluded

without incident. Some nine thousand people filled the city's indoor coliseum for the last meeting, and 2,317 of them made public commitments to Jesus Christ.

But the Shining Path guerrillas were ready for Luis that night. As he walked out of the stadium, he shook hands and took several notes people handed to him. *More prayer requests,* Luis thought as he stuffed the papers in his notebook. *I'll look through them later tonight.* Luis and the rest of the crusade team returned to the hotel. They were flying to Lima tomorrow, but tonight was time to celebrate the spiritual harvest. After a time of joyful singing, Luis grabbed a sandwich. One bite later, he started glancing through the notes he had received at the stadium.

Suddenly, Luis stood. "Everybody, listen to this. It's from the Shining Path." Into the tense silence, Luis read the message, "Get out of Peru within twenty-four hours or die a painful dog's death."

The team jumped into action. "Should we drive across the border?" someone asked. "Maybe we should immediately cancel the crusade," another suggested. The local crusade committee begged Luis to stay and continue with the meetings in Lima despite the threat.

Luis agreed. "We can't quit now and go home with our tails between our legs. We must press on!"

That night, Luis tossed and turned on his bed. *What do they mean by a painful dog's death?* Luis wondered. *I sure don't want to find out!* As morning dawned, Luis looked out the windows of the old Spanish-style hotel and asked himself, "Will this be my last day on earth? Maybe, maybe not. Whatever happens, I know I will finish my days on earth on God's timetable, not man's."

The crusade meetings at Lima's Alianza Stadium

proceeded as planned, the team taking every security precaution possible. Suddenly, the audience heard a series of explosions. The stadium lights flickered. The more than thirty thousand people gasped.

The terrorists are destroying Lima's electrical power plants, Luis realized. *They're trying to shut us down. If we lose power, scores of people could lose their lives or be severely hurt in the ensuing pandemonium.*

Darkness covered Lima. In an instant, the entire city lost its electrical power. . .except the neighborhood surrounding the Alianza Stadium. Luis took a deep breath, then continued preaching with an increased sense of urgency. *People need to trust Christ now,* Luis thought, *before it's too late!*

The last two crusade meetings were rescheduled for the afternoon. Despite the last-minute time change, forty thousand people packed the stadium on the closing day of the crusade, and more than three thousand people committed their lives to Christ.

Shortly after the crusade in Peru, Luis and Pat joined Kevin and Keith at Wheaton College in Illinois. *Today my sons are graduating, and with honors,* Luis said to himself. His thoughts traveled back over the years, memorable moments flashing through his mind. Looking at his grown sons, Luis was filled with pride. What a special privilege to have been chosen to speak to the graduating class on this day. Joining him on the platform was vice-president and presidential candidate George Bush, who would speak to the undergraduate class.

The following month, Luis spoke to tens of thousands in Switzerland, Denmark, England, France, The Netherlands, and Norway. As expected, he found the spiritual soil hard.

Trying to do mass evangelism in Western Europe was like pulling teeth. Still, more than 2,830 people registered public commitments to Jesus Christ. Then came a three-week national crusade in Argentina, which brought a revival of biblical Christianity to the country.

Back at home again, Luis poured himself into final preparation for the team's first Asian crusade two months later. "Although the gospel is universal, my presentation is not," he told Pat. "My messages are geared for Europeans and Hispanics. With our upcoming crusade in Singapore, I need to try to understand the Chinese mind, but that's no easy task for a Western-trained person. I don't want to make any cultural mistakes while I'm a guest in that country."

Luis had a strategy. He attended Chinese conferences, interviewed Chinese Christian leaders, and then thoroughly studied the books they recommended.

Finally, Asia '86 was underway. As Luis preached in the National Stadium of Singapore, his messages were simultaneously translated into eight major Asian languages and broadcast throughout the continent via a radio and video network. The meetings themselves were attended by more than one-third of a million people with 11,902 people publicly giving their lives to the Lord Jesus Christ. And untold thousands were won to Christ in dozens of other nations through the broadcasts. What a divinely given, glorious privilege for a South-American-born follower of Jesus Christ.

Suddenly the door to Asia swung wide open as Luis received invitations for crusades in Hong Kong, India, Indonesia, Japan, the Philippines, Thailand, and other Asian nations.

But first, Luis had to answer the call to proclaim the gospel in the South Pacific.

twenty-four

The scandal erupted in March of 1987, while Luis was in the middle of four weeks of crusades in Fiji and New Zealand. A group of secular reporters broke the news about the fall of "televangelists" Jimmy and Tammy Bakker.

Taking a much-needed break from his full crusade itinerary, Luis sat in his hotel room discussing the situation with team member Dave Jones. "We've already survived a firestorm of controversy," Luis said. "I still have a hard time believing those four bishops, leaders in New Zealand, would release such a scorching series of accusations against our theology, our methods, and our motives."

"Thank God their plan backfired," Dave said.

"Yes, the public stuck with us through that one. But what effect will this scandal have on us?"

"Already several journalists here have contacted us," Dave responded. "They want to interview you about what happened." The ringing of the phone interrupted the pair's sober dialogue. Dave reached over and lifted the receiver.

"I need to speak to Luis immediately," a woman's voice on the other end declared.

Through a series of quick questions, Dave determined the woman did indeed need to speak to Luis. "It's Sura Rubenstein," Dave said as he handed over the receiver.

Luis immediately remembered the religion writer for the *Oregonian,* one of America's twenty-five largest newspapers. Previously, she had spent several weeks doing an indepth investigation on Luis and the ministry—examining the audited financial records, interviewing anyone she wanted, asking any question she wanted, and observing the team in action at the office and during one of their crusades. She had seemed a bit surprised when Luis gave her free rein in her investigation, especially after she admitted she wasn't a Christian.

After a hurried greeting, Sura explained why she had called. "Luis, the Bakker scandal could end up tarnishing the reputation of other evangelists, unless we act quickly. I want to interview you right now as an excuse to write a big story tonight, making it clear your team is absolutely above reproach."

Luis concurred. *It's a bit ironic,* he thought as he answered her questions. *We've been praying for Sura's salvation for months, and here she is trying to protect our reputation!* As he reviewed the papers the next few days, Luis praised God that all the media in New Zealand—not only Sura—had defended the team's name. *It's just as well,* Luis said to himself. *Running from event to event, as many as six a day, has left me drained. I doubt I would have had any energy to spare on a battle of that magnitude.* God used even people who didn't claim to know Him to protect Luis and the team.

The long, hard-driving days of ministry also exhausted his voice box. Luis began to wonder if his voice would last the entire four weeks on the island. What kept him going were the souls saved: the New York City Marathon women's record-holder, the twenty-one-year-old rebellious daughter of an executive committee member, New Zealand's fifth-ranked professional golfer, the committee-appointed crusade photographer, the prime minister of a South Pacific nation. By the time he left New Zealand, 11,426 other people had publicly committed their lives to Jesus Christ!

Back in the States, one young seminary student was brimming with enthusiasm. "I want to preach to crowds," he told Luis. "I want to be an evangelist and win souls to Christ. How did you get your big break to hold mass crusades?"

"There are no big breaks in mass evangelism," Luis replied. "God leads in many small ways, and we learn obedience each time. Big doors open on small hinges. If you feel God has called you to serve, be faithful to do everything He shows you to do. Sometimes that means preaching the gospel to a small group of men behind bars in a state penitentiary. Sometimes that means speaking at a presidential prayer breakfast. You can't do one without doing the other. Remember the Bible tells us that 'he who is faithful in a very little is faithful also in much' " (Luke 16:10 RSV).

Luis reminded the young man that he would encounter difficulties. "Every evangelist must beware of the four big temptations of pride, immorality, money, and giving up," he said. "Whatever we do, God calls us to walk in the light by the power of His Holy Spirit."

That summer, Luis had another chance to learn to be faithful in following God. He crossed the border into a communist country. On the July Fourth weekend, he didn't see any pyrotechnic displays light the sky, but he experienced his own inward fireworks. They shot off in his stomach during several tense border crossings and a long drive along unfamiliar roads in Eastern Europe.

Finally arriving at Poland's southern border, Luis was warmly welcomed by Christian brothers he had never met before. Seeing the tent they had erected near one of Poland's most densely populated industrial areas, Luis remembered how he had hauled a tent around Argentina for the sake of the gospel many years ago.

More than six hundred people made public commitments to Jesus Christ in what proved to be the largest evangelistic tent meetings within the Eastern bloc to that point. *We are on the verge of seeing God do great things in Eastern Europe,* Luis thought. *Soon we will see thousands come to Jesus Christ.* Little did he know he would soon witness the fall of the Iron Curtain and personally see more than 101,000 Eastern Europeans commit their lives to the Lord within the next four years!

twenty-five

Flying back from Hong Kong, Luis and Pat couldn't stop talking about the marvelous things they had just witnessed. "When I looked out on National Stadium, I couldn't see an empty seat," Luis said. "The crusade guys say we had up to forty-five thousand people there at a time. The harvest we saw last year in Singapore was tremendous, but nothing like the Hong Kong crusade. More than 31,265 people made commitments of faith!"

They began to relate the stories they had heard during the eight-day crusade. Pat remembered how a communist college professor came one night and received Christ as Savior on the spot. Then Luis recalled the high-ranking communist official who had attended several meetings and was absolutely astounded that so many people would take a public stand for Jesus Christ and confess God openly.

"You know, Luis, we've been at this twenty-one years now," Pat finally said. "We've traveled throughout Latin

America and Europe and seen thousands upon thousands make decisions for Christ. But this crusade has to be our new 'benchmark.' "

"I agree," Luis replied. "The Hong Kong crusade always will remind me of what God can do in a nation, and certainly will remain one of the highlights of our ministry."

With the arrival of 1988 came a growing realization. *We truly are an international ministry,* Luis thought. *This year alone we have evangelistic rallies and crusades scheduled in eight countries.*

Preaching first at back-to-back crusades in Mexico, Luis then went on to Denmark. Summer brought speaking engagements at three evangelism leadership conferences. Flying to Washington, D.C., for the Lausanne-sponsored Leadership '88 conference, and then to Los Angeles for the International Congress for the Evangelization of the Latin World was no problem. But Luis almost didn't make it to the third conference.

Just eight days before leaving, Luis received some surprising news from Jakarta, Indonesia. "One of the conference organizers called us, Luis," one team member told him. "Before you leave, you have to obtain a special visa."

"Why didn't they mention this earlier?" Luis asked, a bit perplexed.

"Normally this visa isn't required, but a cult has stirred up problems. Indonesian officials decided to require this document if someone is coming to their country to speak at a religious conference that could have a 'nationwide impact.' "

The team immediately began to pray as Luis submitted the necessary paperwork. Many friends and churches also were asked to take the matter before the Lord. Then came the long wait. A week later, Luis packed his suitcase. "Lord, You know we're leaving tomorrow morning," Luis prayed. "I still don't have my visa. I'm a bit concerned, but I have confidence that You will work out Your perfect will."

When Luis arrived at the office the next day, he immediately asked if his visa had come. The response: "Not yet, Luis."

He kept waiting and praying. "Lord, You know I'm going to have to leave soon." Still the visa didn't come.

Just before Luis had to leave for the Portland International Airport, an express mail courier drove up to the LPEA office. His visa had arrived! If it had come two hours later, Luis would have missed his flight. And he would have missed out on ministering to nearly four thousand evangelists, pastors, and other Christian leaders at Indonesia's first national congress on evangelism.

In the fall, after the Palau's youngest son, Steve, headed off for his first year of studies at Wheaton College, Luis headed off for his first evangelistic crusade in Brazil. Then, in November, a dream came true for Luis.

"Ever since Keith Bentson and I had prayed for the world when I was a young man, I've longed to go to India to preach the pure gospel," Luis told Pat. "I've prayed for opportunities to tell Hindus about God's Son and clearly show that 'no one comes to the Father' except through Him. Now I'm here, in the city of Cuttack, for our Festival of Joy and Hope."

At times during the festival, Luis could almost feel the demonic activity. *I'm not surprised,* he thought. *You can't expect anything less when there are three thousand Hindu temples in the area.* During one meeting, Luis suddenly stopped preaching. *Something is definitely wrong here,* he told himself. *Either Satan is at work or some of the professing Christians here are secretly living in serious sin.* Luis told the crowd of his impression, then began to pray. Instantly, the spiritual atmosphere around the Cuttack coliseum cleared, and Luis resumed preaching.

In five days, more than 4,100 made public commitments to Jesus Christ—a tremendous harvest in a city where perhaps three thousand Christians had been.

twenty-six

My heart keeps turning toward America," Luis told Pat in between the flurry of crusades in 1989. "I feel I can no longer ignore America while seeking to call other nations to Jesus Christ. It isn't an either/or situation. Our team must do both."

"What about Billy Graham?" Pat asked. "You always said you wouldn't concentrate on evangelizing America until Billy started slowing down."

"I really believe that God wants me in America, but I won't make another move before talking to Billy." But for some reason, Luis felt nervous about calling the older evangelist.

A couple of weeks later while in Los Angeles, Luis received a phone call. With a start, he realized that the voice belonged to none other than Billy Graham.

"I just saw that article in *Christianity Today*," Billy told Luis.

Thinking quickly, Luis recalled the write-up that reported on recent Palau crusades in Poland and Hungary, and discussed an invitation the team had accepted to preach the gospel in the first public stadium evangelistic crusades in the history of the Soviet Union.

"Goodness gracious!" Billy exclaimed. "You're all over the world these days."

Luis took a deep breath, then said, "Billy, I've got to ask you something." He explained about his longtime burden for America. "I feel the time has come that I should accept more crusade invitations in the States and really go for the bigger cities. But I want to feel that I have your full blessing."

Billy said, "Well, you don't need it. But if you want it, you've got it. Get on with it! Everybody talks about evangelizing America. Now let's really do it."

That April, following the team's eighth crusade in the United States in eight years, the board of directors mandated that the Luis Palau Evangelistic Association start accepting invitations for as many as four American crusades each year.

"How ironic," Luis said to himself. "On the heels of this momentous decision, we'll be just about everywhere else but America in 1989." And off he went to Wales for five weeks of crusade meetings, then to the Philippines for the Lausanne II in Manila Congress on World Evangelization, where he received twenty-five more invitations for crusades.

In the middle of August, Luis and several other team members boarded a plane to Bogotá, Colombia. As they flew south, their prayers for safety flew heavenward. Their trip followed on the heels of forty-eight hours of political assassinations ordered by the cocaine cartel. Even the leading presidential candidate was gunned down in public.

All-out war had been declared. In the middle of the killings, arson, explosions, and machine-gun fire, Luis preached to capacity crowds in the capital city. The final meeting, however, almost ended in disaster.

Luis looked around the eighteen thousand seat stadium in amazement. About twenty-three thousand people crammed into every available space and more than six thousand crowded outside. "I heard they had to lock the stadium doors and gates during the crusade service," he said to the secret service agent assigned to protect him. The agent had left his side for a moment earlier, but had quickly returned. It seemed that the guard was sticking even closer to Luis than before, if that were possible. Luis had no idea that the police had discovered arson equipment and materials in the stadium. Apparently, some thugs had planned to set the whole thing off during the meeting that Sunday evening. A firebomb, capacity crowds, and locked doors would have made for a nightmare of catastrophic proportions.

The next morning, the secret service agent told Luis about the scare. "When I found out what the police had discovered," he told Luis, "I left your side and went straight to my wife. She came last night with our baby. I told her, 'There's going to be trouble. Go home. I don't want to have to decide between helping you and the man I'm assigned to protect.' "

Thankfully, the crusade ended without incident, and that week an amazing 10,288 people committed their lives to Jesus—including the secret service agent.

A few weeks later, Luis traveled to the Soviet Union for a historic series of crusades in four republics. He had dreamed for years of preaching in cities like Moscow, Leningrad, Kiev, Riga, and Kishinev. But to actually have official government permission to preach the liberating gospel of Jesus Christ to the masses in Olympic stadiums and other venues was the thrill of a lifetime.

While there, a telegram arrived for Luis. "It's from Billy Graham," he told his team, then read the note aloud: "We are praying that God will abundantly bless you and that many people will find Christ. We are praying that your meetings will help open doors for others that may come later."

What a wonderful friend and father in Christ Billy has always been to us! Luis thought. *We have felt the prayers of God's people every step of the way.*

One day Luis told his interpreter, Viktor Hamm, "I've never seen so much soul-searching in my life. During each meeting I've watched people suddenly weep, sob, even shake almost uncontrollably."

Viktor replied, "People want to confess their sins to God. When you lead them in prayer, say, 'God, forgive my sins. God, forgive my sins.' "

Luis took his suggestion. Sometimes he would say it three times, and each time the volume rose as people prayed along with him. *If only there were this kind of response to the gospel in America,* Luis thought.

When Christmas arrived, Luis and Pat both felt a bit sad. Andrew, their third son, decided to spend the holidays in Boston where he had moved after graduating from the University of Oregon that summer.

"You know, this is our first Christmas without the whole family together since our twins were born," Luis told Pat. But it wasn't Andrew's distance from home that troubled Luis; it was his distance from the Lord. "There's little Pat and I can do now, Lord," Luis prayed. "Andrew is on his own. All we can do is commit him to You, keep the communication lines open, love him, continue praying, and wait."

While 1989 brought an explosive period of evangelism for the team, 1990 would bring a time of extreme opposition from Satan. After months of intense prayer and hard work, the door for crusade evangelism slammed shut in the cities of Vina Del Mar, Chile; Calcutta, India; and Dhaka, Bangladesh.

The cancellations of those crusades one after another pulled Luis to the Scriptures. "Should we pull back and retreat in defeat?" he asked his team. "Hardly! God's Word exhorts us to 'Endure hardship. . .like a good soldier of Christ Jesus' (2 Timothy 2:3). We are told to 'Be strong in the Lord and in his mighty power. Put on the full armor of God so that you can take your stand against the devil's schemes' (Ephesians 6:10–11). We are reminded that 'The weapons we fight with are not the weapons of the world. On the contrary, they have divine power to demolish strongholds' (2 Corinthians 10:4).

"From a human point of view, yes, we've suffered certain setbacks and apparent defeats. But we have no idea of the victories God has in store for us just ahead!"

twenty-seven

U rgency surrounded the request. Romania had just been liberated from the grip of communism. Now Christians wanted to bring spiritual liberation to their country, as well. The newly formed Evangelical Alliance of Romania contacted the team and asked Luis to come for a series of evangelistic crusades.

Upon hearing that it generally took two or three years to make all the necessary preparations, Dr. Paul Negrut and other top Romanian Christian leaders begged Luis to come that spring. With the collapse of dictatorship, a vacuum had been created—in politics, in economics, in culture, and especially in the spiritual realm. "It is absolutely vital that you bring the gospel of Jesus Christ to our people."

Taking a step of faith, the team agreed to go.

Two days after the nation's first free elections in fifty-three years, Luis and his team arrived in Romania. For nine days in three of Romania's largest stadiums, Luis preached the gospel. "You Romanians are now politically free," he told each audience, "but you can also be spiritually free." The response—up to 9,500 coming forward each evening—far exceeded anything Luis had ever imag*ined*. *I can hardly believe the miracle happening before my very eyes,* Luis silently exclaimed. *It's the Book of Acts, Volume II!*

That fall and winter, Luis spoke at crusades in Indonesia, Japan, and Costa Rica, but in his heart he couldn't wait to travel back to Romania the next spring for five more crusades.

The return trip was well worth it, with literally tens of thousands more coming to Christ! Luis would never forget the closing night of their last crusade. After giving the invitation to a packed stadium in the city of Constantsa, he panicked. *Everyone has left his seat to come forward,* Luis thought in amazement. *No, it just looks like everyone. Had they misunderstood?* Quickly, Luis explained the gospel again, then told the sea of people gathered in front of the platform, "If you've just invited Jesus Christ to come into your life, if you've just accepted God's forgiveness of your sins, raise your hand."

Nearly everyone lifted a hand!

That night, excitement kept Luis awake. He kept seeing those 8,200 people—nearly eighty percent of the audience— make commitments to Christ.

A journalist later asked the crusade chairman, "Is this more than you expected?"

His twinkling eyes and big smile answered before he spoke in slightly broken English. "Sure!" he said, laughing. "We are just fifteen hundred evangelicals in Constantsa, a town of half a million people. Just four evangelical churches! What a wonderful and blessed time. After forty-five years of communism, it's incredible to see such a deep desire in the heart of so many people to receive Christ."

Lord, what an incredible finale to a fantastic season of harvesting, Luis prayed as he flew home. *Thank You for giving me the privilege of seeing more than eighty-five thousand Romanians give their lives to Christ.*

That fall, Luis spent a week in San Antonio, Texas. Each evening after the crusade meetings, Luis would hurry to the local television studio. Soon, he was on the air, live, talking with viewers who called in with their questions or concerns. One night, Larry, a thirty-two-year-old man dying of AIDS, was up late watching *The Arsenio Hall Show* on channel 35. The show ended, commercials aired, then Luis appeared on the screen. Larry sat and listened for a few minutes, then picked up the phone.

"I'm going through torture," he told Luis, then broke into tears while on the air. With his own heart aching, Luis counseled Larry, then asked him if he was ready to accept the forgiveness and love, the peace and hope that Jesus Christ offers.

Larry said "yes." Immediately, Luis led a still-tearful Larry in prayer, then welcomed him into the family of God.

Off the air, Larry gave out his address and phone number. The team contacted a solid local church whose trained counselors immediately visited Larry, offering him compassionate, follow-up care. Before his death, Larry repeatedly expressed to them his hope of heaven.

All told, just over three thousand were added to the fold in San Antonio. Another seventeen thousand trusted Christ during crusades in the capital of Bulgaria, in one of Brazil's leading cities, and in two of the most strategic cities in the

Philippines. Traveling as much as he did, Luis made it a point early in his ministry to spend most of December at home. That Christmas was no exception. Pat and Luis celebrated the holidays, marveling that this was their thirtieth Christmas together as a couple and their first as grandparents.

But Andrew was absent again. He decided to stay in Boston, where he worked as a manager in a large department store. In his heart, Luis wondered how long it would be until his third son returned to the fold.

twenty-eight

Three months had passed since Mexico's constitution had been changed, allowing new religious freedoms. But would three months be enough time to erase the hostile attitudes toward the gospel? On his way to the capital city for three week-long crusades, Luis knew he would soon find out.

The familiar hustle and bustle of the capital greeted him when he arrived in Mexico City in the spring of 1992. *I've been crusading in Mexico for twenty-four years now,* Luis realized. *But this trip is the first time I've been recognized as a "distinguished visitor."* Only two religious figures previously had ever been given this honor—the Buddhist Nobel Prize winner Dalai Lama and Pope John Paul II.

Official honor not withstanding, Luis encountered threats of violence and kidnapping, ugly rumors, near cancellation of stadium meetings by midlevel government officials, and the uninformed, biased reporting by the press—schemes of

Satan to stop the advancement of the gospel.

Some government officials and religious leaders cautioned Christians that they were taking advantage of the new religious freedoms too quickly. "Slow down," one official said. Then, for two days during the final week of the crusade, smothering smog blanketed Mexico City. "The news is calling it one of the worst cases of smog in world history, Luis," one of his team members told him. "Officials have enacted emergency measures, restricting traffic, closing factories, and canceling classes. Many people have become sick."

Still, God's Word went forth. Crowds of up to twenty thousand a night attended the ten crusade meetings in two soccer stadiums and a bullring. Luis encouraged Mexico City's Christians to plan a parade after the last crusade meeting. He told them, "We can march downtown and rally at a national monument there in the capital."

They accepted the challenge, but the parade almost didn't happen. An hour before the march was to begin, two courageous pastors—one a doctor, the other a lawyer— verbally sparred with midlevel government officials. "Fine, go ahead and have that parade," one official finally said. Then he added threateningly, "But Monday we'll be seeing you."

That day, hundreds of thousands of Christians filled downtown Mexico City. *The nation's evangelicals are here to stay,* Luis thought triumphantly, *and they are no longer afraid!*

Across the Rio Grande from Texas that September, near capacity crowds filled the baseball stadium on opening night of the crusade in Reynosa. Luis glanced across at Mayor Ramon Perez García seated beside him on the platform. The mayor had gladly accepted his offer to say a few words of welcome that evening. In surprise, Luis listened as Mayor Perez named him guest of honor in front of the fourteen thousand people there.

"What energy we have here!" he commented to Luis.

"It's the energy of God," Luis said.

"Yes, yes," the mayor replied. That night, his wife came forward to receive Christ!

On the other side of the river in McAllen, Texas, Luis proclaimed the gospel to people besieged by occult activity, multimillion-dollar drug deals, and gang violence. Four rallies in Memorial Stadium drew 32,500 people. Thousands more heard the Good News through four nights of live call-in television. Preempting *The Tonight Show with Jay Leno* may have brought complaints from viewers, but in those few hours, nine people prayed on the air to receive Christ. And who could forget the miracle that occurred in the studio when two cameramen and a control room operator trusted Christ, as well.

In the ten days of evangelism in the Rio Grande Valley, more than 5,400 made decisions for Jesus Christ. That fall, thousands more committed their lives to the Lord during crusades in Panama, Portugal, and Phoenix, Arizona. As Luis watched the crowds walk forward during each of those crusades, his heart filled with thanksgiving and joy. But a part of him remained sad. *God has given me this opportunity to preach and to see many come to know Him,* he thought. *There's no greater joy than this. . .but what about my son Andrew? How can my joy be complete until Andrew stands here as one who walks with Christ?*

Then in 1993, Luis prepared to speak at a national crusade in Jamaica. Knowing their third son loved to fish, Luis and Pat called Andrew in Boston. "We'd love for you to join us in Jamaica. Take some vacation time, and fly out to the island. They say the fishing's great here."

Andrew agreed.

While Andrew reeled in marlin, Luis reeled in souls. For fifteen days in eleven cities, Luis proclaimed the gospel, and more than 17,500 made commitments to Christ. One night, Luis spoke at an evangelistic dinner attended by many members of Jamaica's parliament. Several of the country's top leaders trusted Jesus Christ as Savior.

During the final meeting in Kingston, Luis listened as a businessman told the crowd how Jesus Christ had changed his life. *His testimony is not very exciting,* Luis thought, with tears in his eyes. *No "fire in the sky" conversion story, no drastic outward changes of his lifestyle. Yet, here I am, weeping.*

That quiet businessman's story affected at least one other person in the crowd, as well. Andrew Palau left the stadium convinced of his need to confess his sin and receive God's forgiveness. Later that night, as Luis and Pat were packing for the trip home, Andrew burst into his parent's hotel room. "Mom, Dad, I'm coming back to God!" he exclaimed.

God revolutionized Andrew's life. His hunger and enthusiasm for the things of God was immediately evident to Luis. When Andrew moved back to Portland, Luis was thrilled to see the 180-degree turn he had made. One year later, Andrew began working part-time at LPEA (joining brothers Kevin and Keith), while attending graduate school at Multnomah Biblical Seminary (the same school Luis attended thirty-five years before).

Is it first-time repentance and genuine belief? Luis wondered. *Or is it a recommitment to Christ? To me it doesn't matter! My joy is that my son is born of God and bearing the fruit of sonship, being conformed to the likeness of Jesus Christ.*

One day Pat started to ask Andrew, "Is there anything your father and I could have done to—"

"There's no value in thinking about this," Andrew said, interrupting her. "Nothing could have stopped me from going my way. I knew what the Bible said. I knew what you and Dad thought. I had a selfish heart and chose to go my own way."

As Luis thought about Andrew's conversion, he realized, *That's what I'd like to see God do for the people of America. There are thousands of other "Andrews" who need Jesus Christ. We must reach out to them with the gospel of Jesus Christ, and we must reach out now!*

With even more conviction than ever, Luis gave out the good news of Jesus Christ that year in Chile, Taiwan, and Fort Worth, Texas.

One of the six U.S. crusades the team planned for 1994 was in Grand Rapids, Michigan. Bob Bobosky, a friend of Luis and a businessman in Portland, found out about the crusade, and told Luis about his seventy-one-year-old father who wasn't a Christian and who lived in Michigan.

"Why don't you take him to the crusade?" Luis asked Bob.

So Bob hopped on a plane and got his dad to come one night.

Afterward, Luis asked Bob's dad, "Mr. Bobosky, have you given your life to Christ?"

"Yes," he replied.

"When did you do it?"

"Tonight," he said. "You twisted my arm."

Putting his arm around the elderly gentleman, Luis said, "Mr. Bobosky, I'm glad I twisted your arm."

Later, Luis thought, *How I wish I could twist everybody's arm. But of course no one can be coerced into heaven against his or her will. Everyone must choose freely to surrender to Christ.*

Luis flew to Miami for the first crusade of the new year, then it was on to Nepal, the world's only Hindu nation, for the Good News Easter Festival.

One hour into Nepal's first evangelistic crusade meeting, Luis and his interpreter stepped up to the lectern to speak. Before Luis could finish his first sentence, however, the power went off, shutting down the sound system. A generator the team had brought failed to provide sufficient power, and a few people in the crowd got up to leave. Fifteen minutes later, a pair of 100-watt speakers were hooked up to the generator. Luis began to speak to the 7,500 seated on the soccer field.

"At the end of my message, I'm going to give you an invitation to bend the knee to Jesus," he said. "I don't want you to change religions. I want you to fall in love with Jesus, to give your heart to Jesus, to know the one and only Savior of the world and worship Him." More than 430 gave their lives to Jesus Christ that night. All told, the three days of meetings resulted in 1,440 commitments of faith.

In 1996, after four years of preparation, Luis traveled to Chicago for a two-month marathon of evangelistic crusades. The result: 10,100 commitments to Christ. After one men's luncheon in suburban Chicago, an elderly gentleman slowly walked toward Luis. His impaired legs made each step a struggle. He introduced himself then told Luis he was a retired university professor, age seventy-seven, who once had been a candidate for a Nobel Prize.

Luis asked him, "Have you got eternal life, or are you still on the way?"

He replied, "My wife's going to heaven, and I'm going to hell."

That's interesting, Luis thought. *I didn't ask him that.* Then he said, "Professor, why do you say that you're going to hell?"

"When I was a boy, I had faith, and then I lost it," he said. "Now it's too late."

"Professor, it's never too late. Besides, you came to talk to me because you want to know, don't you?"

"Yes," he said, "I do."

"When did you lose your faith?"

"In college. They took it from me at the university, and I've been forty years without faith. God will never take me back."

"Yes. He will take you back."

"No, He won't. . .it's too late."

"Professor, why do you say that?"

"Because I'm so unworthy, that's why. I'm so unworthy."

"Professor, you're right. You are unworthy. But so am I, and so is the rest of the human race." Because it was Holy Week, Luis said, "Why do you think we celebrate Good Friday? The Cross, Professor. On the Cross is where God took care of our guilt and our sin, and He buried it forever. Professor, you really want to be forgiven, don't you?"

"Yes, I do."

"Professor, God can take away your guilt—even forty years' worth. Listen to what He says in the Bible: 'Their sins and their lawless deeds I will remember no more'" (Hebrews 10:17 NKJV).

"That's beautiful," he said.

"Are you ready to be received back by God?"

"I am."

Luis put his arm around him. The professor trembled as he prayed to invite Jesus Christ into his heart.

About two weeks later, at a luncheon for women, Luis told the professor's story. Afterward, an elderly woman stopped Luis and told him, "I'm the professor's wife."

"Did I tell the story right?" Luis asked.

"I don't know; I wasn't there," she said. "But I'll tell you something. My husband is more certain than I am that I'm going to heaven. I'm not certain at all."

"Why do you say you're not certain?" Luis asked.

"Because I've let God down so many times. I've gone to church all my life, but I feel I never quite measure up."

"Madam, if not letting God down is a condition for going to heaven," Luis said, "we've all had it, because we've all let Him down. Heaven is a gift of the mercy of God."

She understood and began to place her hope in God's work on the cross.

Two weeks later, Luis spoke to this couple on the phone. "Thank you," they said, "for pointing the way to assurance of eternal life."

The Say Yes Chicago campaign yielded more than spiritual fruit. Working with a team of evangelists to reach that bustling city with the gospel helped cement in Luis's mind the need to do more to mentor young evangelists. *Why should all our years of experience and our wealth of materials be wasted?* Luis asked himself. *We've discovered what works and what doesn't. Now it's time to help all those guys—the new generation of evangelists—carry the banner of evangelism well into the twenty-first century.*

As a result, in late 1996 the Palau Association unveiled the Next Generation Alliance^sm initiative.

"We've helped many young evangelists over the years,"

202

Luis told his team, "just as Billy Graham and others helped me. But I feel an urgency to do more.

"First," Luis continued, "we'll make ourselves available year-round to mentor a carefully selected group of partner evangelists. This is not an easy day for evangelists. Even in the U.S., most have one, maybe two staff members. And almost all lack the infrastructure to pursue larger crusades. So we'll help. We'll help them pursue open doors for crusade invitations, mobilize and train the church for evangelism, and raise the prayer and financial support they need to keep preaching the gospel.

"Second, we'll schedule training conferences. Over the years, hundreds of people have asked me questions about evangelism—how to evaluate crusade invitations, how to do friendship evangelism and counselor training, how to do Christian fund-raising, how to work with the secular media, and so on. Now we can thoroughly address these important questions.

"Third, we'll offer seminary-level evangelism training. The top leaders at Multnomah Biblical Seminary have agreed to partner with us and have developed a new master's degree in evangelism. It's a terrific program for young people who have a passion for reaching the lost with the good news of Jesus Christ."

On the heels of this new alliance, Luis and the team launched Operation Pacific Northwest. *Now we have the perfect combination,* Luis thought. *With the help of our partner evangelists, we can accept even more crusade invitations anywhere in the region. The size of the town no longer matters.*

Soon, invitations began pouring in from all over the Northwest. One invitation that Luis didn't take seriously, though, was a request from many pastors he knew to do a crusade in Portland. *Anywhere in the U.S. or overseas, great. . .just not in my own home city, please!* Luis thought.

A whirlwind of thirty-three crusades and rallies filled Luis's schedule the next two years. During the spring of 1998, Luis flew to Egypt for his first Middle East campaign where he proclaimed the gospel up and down the Nile to an estimated 110,000 each night.

"Are you sure?" team members asked incredulously. "That's close to half a million people over four days!" But detailed reports confirmed the numbers.

More than three thousand people crammed into Kasr el-Dobara Evangelical Church each of the four nights of the campaign. Then, immediately after each meeting, a videotape of the service was edited, copied, and distributed by volunteer couriers for showings in 574 churches the next day. Again, the churches were full; some even held two services each evening.

On Saturday night as Luis preached, a man called the church and asked for the pastor. "There's a bomb in the church," the man said. "It's going to go off in six minutes." Security signaled Luis who quickly ended his message and gave the invitation. Then they whisked him away in a waiting Jeep. Egyptian church officials, who deal with such threats on a regular basis, told security they had overreacted.

When Luis heard that the estimated number of commitments to Christ surpassed 30,500, he said, "It was absolutely amazing that in a country like Egypt there would be such fabulous openness."

That summer, flying back from the Republic of Palau, in the South Pacific, where more than 1,350 indicated decisions for Jesus Christ, Luis knew he had a decision to make. "What should I do?" he asked God. "You know I'm nervous about accepting the invitation we've received to have a campaign in our home city. If only a few hundred people show up to hear me preach in Onslow, Australia, who would know? But if a crusade in Portland flops big time, my whole community—my church—even the grocery clerk at the local supermarket would know. There will be nowhere to hide!"

As he looked out over Portland from the air, he knew the answer. "Okay, God," Luis said. "We'll do it." But first, it was off to the East Coast.

For an entire month during the spring of 1999, ten other evangelists joined with Luis to proclaim the life-changing gospel of Jesus Christ at more than ninety events up and down the state of Maine.

Despite a reputation as God's "frozen chosen," some ten thousand Christians in New England—mostly in Maine, but also in Massachusetts, New Hampshire, and Vermont—fired up for what newspapers described as the largest outreach in Maine's history. Evangelistic meetings, radio, television, literature, even the Internet blanketed the state with the gospel.

"People told me that New England was too hard," Luis told a *Boston Globe* reporter. "I love a challenge. When people say, 'You can't break through here,' I say, 'Maybe I can't, but God can.' "

And He did! More than 5,600 men, women, youth and children throughout Maine made public commitments to Jesus Christ.

"We can't ignore the God-given success of Mission Maine," Luis later told his team. "Let's make a commitment to partner with other evangelists for state-wide missions each year. Next spring we'll take on the state of North Dakota!"

Soon, invitations started coming in from other states, as well.

Several months later, the Palau team decided to test yet another new strategy for evangelizing America. The plan was straightforward: to hold an outdoor evangelistic music festival. The place: Waterfront Park in Luis's home city. The big question in everyone's mind, however, was: Will anyone come to a Christian event featuring "Great Music, Good News"?

During a press conference that Monday, one reporter asked Luis how many people were expected to attend that weekend. Luis replied, "If ten thousand people come, I'll be very happy. If fifty thousand come, I'll be out of my mind."

Nothing could have prepared Luis for the mass of people—a crowd estimated by police at fifty-five thousand—that crammed into a five-block section of Waterfront Park along the Willamette River in downtown Portland that Saturday evening.

"God, it's tremendous!" Luis prayed. "This crowd tonight, plus the thirty-eight thousand who attended the night before. I'm delirious with joy! The festival has gone far beyond what I had even hoped. It's ironic, God, because I got my start evangelizing in the parks and streets of Argentina years ago. Now, all these years later, You seem to be telling my team and me to go to where the people are here in America. Thank You, God, for opening a new door for us to reach the bigger cities in an exciting new way."

The years ahead hold many more crusades, state-wide missions, and festivals for Luis and his team. Even after thirty-three years of ministry, after preaching the gospel to thirteen million people in sixty-eight nations, he's not ready to quit. Luis figures he can preach until at least age ninety-two.

"In coming years, I'm committed to continuing to do all I can to call America and the nations to Christ," Luis says. "The opportunities today are boundless. I hope you'll join me!"

About the Author

Author Ellen Bascuti worked as an associate editor for the Luis Palau Evangelistic Association for six years. She wishes to express her thanks to Luis Palau, who graciously permitted use of his autobiography *Luis Palau: Calling America and the Nations to Christ* (copyright 1994 by Luis Palau), interviews, radio programs, and other materials in the writing of this book.